"In this taut, fearless ~~and~~ ~~well~~
Larry Ward offers
America's racial kai
ally and collectively
and transformed. L ~~~~ ~~~~ ~~~~
trauma theory, neuroscience, and years of practice …
the result is a searing, liberative, and tender work."
—Jan Willis, author of *Dharma Matters*

"An extraordinary gift of generosity.… *America's Racial Karma* doesn't just add to the essential conversation around race, racialization, and discrimination, but rather redefines the very conversation itself from the inside out."
—Brother Phap Hai, author of *Nothing to It*

"I know Larry Ward's teachings, firsthand, to have come from his humble, dedicated, devoted, long and steady practice. Wise, clear, heartfelt, and based on his own authentic transformative experience … sure to be a classic among those who are serious about awakening."
—Zenju Earthlyn Manuel, author of *The Deepest Peace*

"Dr. Larry Ward is an elder in American Buddhism, using his decades of heart-centered practice to guide our community into a deeper and more relevant exploration of America's struggle with racism in order to support us in our healing ... an invitation to us to tend to our own hearts as we disrupt deeply ingrained thoughts and actions that have perpetuated the violence of America's racial karma. We will all be much freer because of Dr. Ward's teaching."
—Lama Rod Owens, author of *Love and Rage*

"Welcome medicine for today's generation of decolonial, spirit-led seekers and activists."
—Katie Loncke, codirector of the Buddhist Peace Fellowship

"Buddhism is syncretic and malleable and has always mingled with whatever culture it has landed within, whether in Tibet, Japan, or China. So why not in America? More importantly for us, Larry Ward is able to relate Buddhism to the experience of people of color in America. We need this."
—Rajeev Balasubramanyam, author of *Professor Chandra Follows His Bliss*

"Rich in practice in the Plum Village Buddhist tradition, *America's Racial Karma* is a must-read book to understand our individual and collective legacy and to walk the long path toward reconciliation and awakening." —Valerie Brown, coauthor of *The Mindful School Leader*

"Accessible to those experienced in meditation practices and beginners alike, Larry Ward's book offers us a way to bring clear intention and compassionate action to our path of racial healing with concrete practices to help us come back again and again to healing ever-deeper layers of our embodied, psychological racial traumas. A refuge for today and future generations." —Marisela B. Gomez, MD/PhD, author of *Race, Class, Power, and Organizing in East Baltimore*

"The living tradition of Buddhism will only progress if it reflects and includes the diversity of insight and experiences from a spectrum of teachers. Dr. Larry Ward is an important voice for our collective awakening." —Denise Nguyen, executive director of the Thich Nhat Hanh Foundation

"Toward the project of national healing, Larry Ward brings to bear his decades of experience to instruct us on locating the seeds of racialization within us all. Brimming with aphorisms of wisdom, Ward shows us how to build a society of belonging."
—john a. powell, author of *Racing to Justice*

"Preacher, poet, griot, and Zen Master, Larry Ward shows us how we can each manifest our inherent wholeness in the midst of the brokenness of white supremacy." —Kaira Jewel Lingo

"Timely and timeless … healing and transformation from a wise elder committed to our collective liberation." —Julio Rivera, founder of the meditation app Liberate

"In clear, courageous words, the author reveals America's racial karma and its linkages to unbridled greed for wealth and power. Dr. Ward shows how Buddhist psychology can help us confront racism and heal its trauma within our own body-mind."
—Robertson Work, author of
A Compassionate Civilization

AMERICA'S RACIAL KARMA

Also by
Larry Ward and Peggy Rowe Ward

Love's Garden:
A Guide to Mindful Relationships

America's Racial Karma

An Invitation to Heal

Larry Ward, PhD

PARALLAX PRESS

BERKELEY, CALIFORNIA

Parallax Press
Berkeley, California
parallax.org
Parallax Press is the publishing division of the Plum Village Community of
Engaged Buddhism, Inc.
© 2020 by Larry Ward
All rights reserved
Author photograph by Jovelle Tamayo, courtesy of *Tricycle: The Buddhist
Review*
The White Man's Burden (Apologies to Rudyard Kipling) by Victor Gillam,
public domain
Cover and text design by Zoe Norvell
Printed in Canada on 100 percent recycled paper

ISBN 978-1-946764-74-4
E-book ISBN 978-1-946764-75-1

Library of Congress Cataloging-in-Publication Data
Names: Ward, Larry, 1948, author.
Title: America's racial karma : an invitation to heal / Larry Ward, PhD.
Description: Berkeley, California : Parallax Press, 2020. |
Includes bibliographical references.
Identifiers: LCCN 2020025947 (print) | LCCN 2020025948 (ebook) |
ISBN 9781946764744 (trade paperback) | ISBN 9781946764751 (epub)
Subjects: LCSH: United States--Race relations. | Racism--United States. |
 Karma--United States. | Buddhism--United States.
Classification: LCC E184.A1 W23 2020 (print) | LCC E184.A1 (ebook) |
DDC 305.800973--dc23
LC record available at https://lccn.loc.gov/2020025947
LC ebook record available at https://lccn.loc.gov/2020025948
1 2 3 4 5 / 24 23 22 21 20

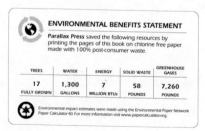

ENVIRONMENTAL BENEFITS STATEMENT

Parallax Press saved the following resources by
printing the pages of this book on chlorine free paper
made with 100% post-consumer waste.

TREES	WATER	ENERGY	SOLID WASTE	GREENHOUSE GASES
17 FULLY GROWN	1,300 GALLONS	7 MILLION BTUs	58 POUNDS	7,260 POUNDS

Environmental impact estimates were made using the Environmental Paper Network
Paper Calculator 4.0. For more information visit www.papercalculator.org.

Our racial suffering
is deep and wide.
It is a particular
kind of *samsara*.
Repeated cycles
of bitterness, pain,
and fear.

It is sustained
by our conditioning,
both individual
and collective.

It is the undercurrent
of a failed paradigm
of aggression, ownership
of peoples, and
enduring institutionalized
racism.

This failed paradigm
of views presents us
with a profound opportunity
to rebuild the shape
of our thinking, speech, and
action as we can
and must redefine
what it means to be a human being.

Contents

Introduction

❀

An Invitation
to Heal

Race has been a source of trouble in human affairs since the contours of the modern ways of thinking about it became dimly visible in the rise of new scientific ideas about human beings as parts of the natural world.

KWAME ANTHONY APPIAH

✤

My growing years took place in Cleveland, Ohio, on the East Side of the city near Lake Erie. It was a predominantly African American neighborhood in the 1950s, with a few European immigrants from Polish and Italian roots. Interactions between children and adults of different races, other than on the job or through commercial transactions, were controlled and rare. To my young eyes, members of the community moved about their days going to work, to church, and to school in a kind of stunned silence about race, as if hoping that by never acknowledging it, the bitterness just under the surface would not leak out. Even then, I sensed we were all wrapped in a blanket of fear and yearning.

The nightly news of my teenage years expanded its coverage to voices echoing the pain of centuries, determined to be silent no more. Many of these voices and their stories became focal points in the story of race in the United States, including those of Rosa Parks, Angela Davis, Dr. Martin Luther King Jr., Malcolm X, and Dennis Banks.

As a Black man writing about race in America, I do not forget the first peoples of this land, their genocide, and their continued presence. Many of us tend to think of African American bodies when we think about America and race, yet the story of racial hierarchy in this country began long before the arrival of African people on these shores. Now, we find ourselves living in a racialized world that existed before we were born, and our minds have been conditioned to see race as real. This racialized awareness permeates us like a disease of the psyche, cementing our minds to a system of social worth and value by skin pigmentation. It animates our thinking, speech, and behavior individually and collectively. It influences our attitudes, emotional states, habitual dispositions, and social organization. How has this mindset become so powerful?

From my childhood in the fifties to the era of the war in Vietnam in the sixties, when Dr. King and Thich Nhat Hanh found in each other a source of spiritual friendship and political solidarity, and the many domestic and international conflicts in which race has played a part, in my own lifetime the cycle of America's racial karma has become very visible. As I grew into adulthood, I was fortunate to have the chance to observe many peoples and places around the world, with jobs that took me around the globe to factories, educational institutions, consulting firms, churches, and community development efforts, in rural villages as well as urban centers. On most occasions, I've noticed the presence of racialized consciousness in the thinking, speech, and behaviors not only in myself but also in the people around me.

The first time I went to work in Asia many years ago, I was part of a faculty running trainings in new methodologies for schoolteachers in Hong Kong. My first day on the job, I had someone come up to me wanting to know if I was the luggage carrier for the team. I said, "No, I'm the dean." You could see their face working hard to try to fit me into their picture of the world. That's when I knew this racial hierarchy system is global. I've been all over this planet a hundred times, and everywhere I've been, this is an issue. It's such an issue that as an African American going to Africa, people in Africa consider me "white" because I come from the United States. In the sixties and seventies, being regarded as "white" under the yoke of white supremacy gave Black Americans in the Back to Africa movement the shock of their lives. Everybody was clear that white people rule.

Millions of years of adaptation have formed our discriminative intelligence into a complex classification machine that constantly evaluates threats to our safety and integrity. But the kind of thinking that elevates some humans and devalues others based on skin color is not baked into our neurobiology. Some call it racism and colorism; some call it the colonial mind; others call it capitalism; whatever we may call it, those of us who feel the oppressive edge of bias tend to recognize its presence.

I appreciate your opening this book because I know it takes a certain conscious courage to read anything related to the word "race" in the title, because there are few other words in the English language that can activate our autonomic nervous systems so quickly. I am also aware that it is no small task to attempt to describe America's racial karma—what it is, and how to transform it—especially if, many days, it may feel as if there is little or no movement forward. Yet, I know once we recognize America's racial karma as actions that continue to give birth to the notion of white racial superiority and its psychosocial consequences, we gain the necessary insight to change course. We will rage and grieve, but we will also begin to heal.

Of course, race isn't the only knife we use to separate ourselves from each other. All kinds of social inequities around gender, class, ability, and sexuality combine to form unique forms of discrimination and prejudice. The following example from my family is close to my heart. Twenty-five years ago, I was in a remote area of Costa Rica when my mother passed away. I hurriedly made arrangements to go home to Cleveland for her funeral rites. When I arrived at my old house, a young man I didn't recognize was exiting our door, his face wet with tears. I asked who he was and discovered Tim, a long-lost cousin.

Why the tears? "Why are you leaving?" I asked. He said, "Your father won't let me stay here because I'm gay." I was appalled. I went upstairs to confront my father. He said it was a religious matter. "If Tim cannot stay here, neither will I," I said, and Tim and I immediately went to stay at my sister's house.

Such is the deep-seated power of prejudice that it can overcome the sense of familial belonging, even in times of grief. I'm glad to say that my precious father's biases did become less rigid—he became less of a bigot—and he did become more open and respectful toward Tim. My father's behavior painfully exemplifies the kind of cognitive bias that distorts our thinking, decisions, and actions toward others, often causing them physical or emotional harm.

After living many years outside of the United States, in the year 2011, my wife, Peggy, who is white, and I relocated to progressive Asheville, North Carolina, to start a small business and develop a community of spiritual practice. After settling into our new home, we were invited by Gail Williams O'Brien to lead a meditation retreat in the college town of Chapel Hill on the other side of the state. This connection was made through our association with Zen Master

Thich Nhat Hanh and the Plum Village Community of Engaged Buddhism; Gail is a history professor emerita at the University of North Carolina at Chapel Hill and the author of *The Color of the Law: Race, Violence, and Justice in the Post–World War II South*.

On the six-hour drive from Asheville to Chapel Hill to meet Gail, I was at first startled by the presence of Confederate flags flying from many homes and businesses along the way. My sense of shock gave way to an increasing uneasiness within my body and mind, compounded each time I encountered a Confederate flag on the decals of a vehicle in front of me. Visible through my car windows were subtle and not-so-subtle reminders of Jim Crow attitudes and America's habits of racial dissociation and aversion. There seemed to be a rhythm of daytime integration and nighttime segregation. While some of the overt patterns of segregation had changed, it was clear to me that the psychological wounds of the past remained unhealed.

Stopping at gas stations, the politeness Peggy and I did experience seemed constrained, with furtive eye contact. The air was filled with discomfort, and I felt like an alien in my home country. My sympathetic nervous system went on high alert. My heart raced; I had knots in my stomach; and memories rose up within me of past trips to the South in the 1970s, in which my life had been threatened. My mind was filled with concerns for our safety. I had left the United States to work abroad for decades, but on returning, I was filled with the same fear from my childhood and teen years. Why did I, a grown man, not feel safe in 2011—three years into the Obama presidency—in my home country? On election night in 2008, the moment we saw the televised results, I'd turned to Peggy and said, "Shit's going to hit the fan," because I knew that the election results would activate the hatred that had sent me outside of America for so many years.

The anger, sadness, and disgust I was carrying revealed themselves to me later during our community meditation. My body and mind began to calm down. I looked deeper into my experience and realized that I was witnessing the impact in myself of a society built on the sinking sands of the white supremacy complex. I began to see how all of us—regardless of how we or our ancestors came to be here—have been conditioned to live on this land as forever strangers. Later, after a meal, we discussed the importance of Gail's book as well as our new life in Asheville, and we managed to return to some equanimity and enjoy our visit.

Nevertheless, I woke up the next morning with a question on my heart and mind. Why is the notion of racialized consciousness, with white skin on the throne of the human species, so intractable in the hearts and minds of many? Despite its trail of suffering around the world—for colorism is not unique to America—why does it persist? Movements, martyrs, and magistrates had not set us free from this great social-psychological construction.

The idea of America's *collective* karma arose within me and inspired me to talk with people wherever I went about the subject of race and its effect on our consciousness. The themes of this book were born from a decade of such talks.

Ten years prior to my and Peggy's trip to see Professor Gail, I had been introduced to Buddhist psychology while taking a retreat with my teacher Thich Nhat Hanh in Plum Village, France. His book on the subject, now known as *Understanding Our Mind,* had a different name back then: *Transformation at the Base.* This title gives us a good clue as to what is required for radical shifts in consciousness. Transformation at the base affects the roots of our body and mind. This is why we practice.

With this lens of Buddhist psychology, I began to see a fresh way to understand the lived experience of consciousness as a dynamic and multilayered reality. I began to see how deeply embedded the idea of race is as the psychological base of modern self and society. It's entwined with our notion of ourselves surviving within a world of fear, conflict, and competition, and painful though it may be to hold on to it, without awareness, we cannot let it go.

Not everything has an answer. Some things are not fixable. So, I'm not talking about fixing our racial karma. I'm talking about bending the trajectory and transforming the energy that sustains it. What we've seen in the last few years is the great feeding of animosity and the joy of bigotry. Nothing can live without food. If it's not fed, it will not live.

Echoing the Buddha's model of the mind, Sigmund Freud and others have revealed that we are beings subject to subconscious processes influencing our thinking, speech, and behaviors. Repression and denial of our unconscious mind leads to pathology, or as the Buddha would call it, suffering. Unless we choose to live more deeply than shallow awareness allows, it can be difficult to see what I mean by America's racial karma and observe its turning. We will need to look beyond our contented shallowness and into the roots of our racialized consciousness if we truly desire to heal and transform our past, present, and future.

As students of the Dharma, we know our collective awareness is ultimately impermanent. Ideas that seem set in stone and immovable may in fact change; in fact, they are bound to change. If we look deeply into the mind and body's role in creating, nurturing, and protecting our racialized awareness and its actions, we see an opportunity for transformation. America's racial karma invites us to be attentive to our hearts' conditioning. It invites us to embrace our shared racial trauma at its roots and heal our compromised social imagination, so we may be the ones who come through the mists of racial ignorance into what we may call a good society.

For months after my visit to Gail, I continued to reflect on my question: What lies at the roots of this social construction of racial hierarchy? I began to recognize a kind of catharsis, a sense of energy more like worship, a quality of transcendence that a religion would provide surrounding the notion of white supremacy. I then began to understand its seductive conditioning power and subsequent seeming intractability in history and in the present.

This book and the practices I share invite us to go deeper into our collective psyche and see how it creates a social psychology that nurtures it, which in turn keeps feeding the institutions that damage us so intimately.

America's Racial Karma explores the psychological factors that continue to create our racialized consciousness and the waves of suffering in its wake. Our racialized consciousness is the greatest achievement of white supremacy. It's an example of how human consciousness can be nurtured to perfection in unwholesome ways. It is a fundamental obstacle to the achievement of collective wellness and justice in US society.

For nonwhite people, racialized consciousness is kept alive daily through everyday acts of violence and macrosystemic and micropersonal aggressions. This kind of violence is remote to many white people as members of the group that benefits from racial inequity. I have a friend, Henry, a white man who is sincerely seeking to deepen his understanding of the racial divide in America. In conversation with him, I came to see how his life experience had left him profoundly unprepared for the work of awakening and transformation. Henry is an aware and progressively engaged person, yet for him it is a genuine struggle to understand the distinction between personal racial intention and the social-psychological impact of five hundred years of the system of white supremacy. I write *America's Racial Karma* not only for myself but also for him.

I initiated a special daily routine in the past year while writing this manuscript. Like many of us, I scan the world news every day. Similar to doing a body scan in mindfulness meditation, I go continent by continent, to remember I am a part of something larger than my ego; this is part of my everyday spiritual practice. Every day, my heart gets both broken and restored. I've yet to meet a day when something from the ridiculous to the horrifying does not occur in relationship to race in America.

An NAACP lawsuit over the use of Confederate symbols in public schools, an increase in assaults of Asians nationwide after Donald Trump calls COVID-19 "the Chinese virus," the pandemic causing disproportionately high rates of illness and death in Native, Latinx, and Black communities—and on it goes.

The stories we tell ourselves and one another about race are full of political emotional manipulation, the social theater of status and, most of all, unprocessed trauma. While such stories must be reported for as long as they continue to occur, the unwitting ingestion of them as forms of cultural reenactment actually prevents many of us from the personal and collective work of grieving our racial karma, restoring our racial sanity, and reimagining our lives together. By telling and retelling such stories of suffering, without mindfulness or insight, we reinforce our fears and biases through the triggering and retriggering of our autonomic stress responses.

Storytelling is an ancient means of creating individual and collective identity, but stories are not innocent; they provide language and leave footprints in the cave of the heart that reveal how to be human.

Our racialized stories tend to be in-group affirming and out-group shaming—self-affirming and other-demeaning. Stories of our racialized consciousness are passed from generation to generation and from land to land. We can track the progress of these stories over five hundred years of colonial history as they provided legal, religious, social, and psychological support and justification for ignorance, injustice, and indifference in America.

To assume that our current racial dysfunction is disconnected from America's continental and Eurocentric past is a delusion of the highest order. Our racial past echoes through the air we breathe and permeates the ground on which we walk. This fragmented consciousness predates our birth but still flows through our neural networks, the veins of our being. When it comes to matters of race in America, we are caught in a cycle of reactivity. Our autonomic nervous systems are on high alert, flooding our bodies with the energies of fight, flight, or freeze. If we can learn to stop and look deeply into these energies, we can discover the courage, connection, and imagination to embody a new world.

This book is also a resource to better understand the mind's grasping, clinging, and attachment to the fiction of race. Our minds seem to enjoy projecting qualities onto others with the aim of elevating ourselves. The result is nothing short of tragic: in a fictional universe, we may make ourselves feel safer, but we lose touch with reality. Some of the reflections in this book can help us learn to recognize, name, and rest these mental gymnastics. We will also look at how we can begin to heal our shared racial trauma with awareness, whether we are victims, perpetrators, or witnesses.

Fifty years ago, I had surgery for a knee injury that left me with painful scar tissue. For a long time after my surgery, I lay in bed, immobile. I was like the man in the Bible story who was stuck on his bed just a few feet from a healing pool of waters. Jesus approached him and asked, "How long have you been here?" "Thirty-eight years," the man said, "but no one would help me get in the pool." Jesus asked, "Do you want to get well?" The man said, "Yes," and Jesus's reply was, "Well, get up, pick up your bed, and walk." I had a similar exchange with my knee surgeon post-op. I was well enough to walk, but my mind's resentment at my injured state kept me in bed. My surgeon offered the same words as Jesus to me: "Well, get up and walk." And I did. I thank him each day since then for his encouragement, his belief in me, and also his diagnostic eye.

I see us in America today walking uneasy and contorted from the continuous cycle of actions that create, sustain, and perpetuate our racialized consciousness. This cycle is America's racial karma. For those of us in a deep state of paralysis due to our past pain, shame, grief, and trauma, it's all we can do to exist, get up, and walk.

For many of us, the question becomes: *Am I worthy of being healed?* Feelings of guilt, shame, and grief may seem as solid as blocks of ice within us. Or, the anxiety of our imperfections becoming more exposed paralyzes us from acting and taking the risk to heal. These anxieties are part of the healing process, not obstacles to be feared. To move into healing requires us to be vulnerable. One way I understand this sense of vulnerability is the presence of openness and grace in my body and mind's readiness for change. Anything could happen, and it could even be good.

I have been asking myself as I crafted this book: What do I mean by healing? You may be asking yourself the same question. Many are aware of this sense of racial alienation and denial and the stress it brings daily, while others may walk through their daily life seemingly unaware. Now, I may think I'm okay, and you likely think you're okay too, at least at times. Other times, we may feel broken by what we may witness, experience, or perpetrate on an almost daily basis. It is more than evident that as a society we are not okay. We are burning up and burning out. What rises from the ashes? Our karmic actions. As we walk forward into changing our social institutions and practices, we can also increase our awareness and turn it toward the work of healing.

This book is a journey through our inner and outer lives. In part one, "Deep," the chapter "The Turning Karmic Wheel and the Role of Intention" offers a description of America's repetitive cycle of racial dysfunction and how it came to be. Part two, "Deeper," explores a dynamic understanding of white supremacy and discusses its traumatic effects that still live in our American bones. Part three, "Deeper Still," presents an understanding of healing from Buddhist psychology that will give you the necessary tools for transformation. After "Crossing Mercy's Bridge: Healing the Wounds of Time," the book concludes with a call to the duties of ancestorship not solely as Americans but as full human beings living on this planet Earth.

Part One

❋

Deep

When I Became Currency

When they came for me, I tried to contain my fear
    and my heartbreak.
My bones longed for home as I, sick in the bottom of
a ship, became a dark currency
carried over the sea.

I was sold and sold again, a commodity,
    an instrument of profit seduced and sustained by
    greed, arrogance, and ignorance.
Cold and beleaguered in a new land unknown,
I tried to forget such horror in my bones but the
looks and whispers even to this day remind me:

I am a class of color created by a colonial mind
    missing its own self-worth.
But the dance of my ancestors in my bones have kept
    me awake and kept me alive.
I live beyond such limiting constructs of mind.
I am free because I am not confused.
I am stardust awake.
I am the earth and sky embracing all.

I ride the wind with the eagle and the hawk.

I flow with the rivers into all oceans.

I touch the sun and am touched by the moonlight
like all beings.

I am Nature herself. Awake. Powerful. Resilient.
Generative.

I offer the love of all my ancestors to your ancestors
and the ancestors of all beings.

I offer my presence like rain falling on the wise and
the unwise, the troubled and the untroubled, the just
and the unjust, so that the wounds of time may be
healed in the dance of the flow of birth and death.

1

The Turning Karmic Wheel and the Role of Intention

To accept one's past—one's history—
is not the same thing as drowning in it;
it is learning how to use it.
An invented past can never be used;
it cracks and crumbles under the pressures
of life like clay in a season of drought.

JAMES BALDWIN, *The Fire Next Time*

❦

It started before I was born. It began before you were born, too, this turning wheel of racialized consciousness; its tracks are evident across the face of time and the threads of human connection. Let us propose it is not an intractable condition but a legacy of human thought, speech, and physical behaviors. Our racialized consciousness and the suffering and confusion associated with it need not continue. This moment in our social history compels us to invite ourselves into a path of discoveries, learning, and practices to transform our karma.

I ponder the wheel, an ancient invention of great practicality. Its shape appears throughout human history in art, culture, science, and spiritual traditions. It has provided a powerful image and metaphor for the spiritual journey of humanity. In the Buddhist tradition, the wheel is a primary symbol of an eightfold path of healing and transformation leading to freedom. But the wheel also describes a repeating pattern of suffering called *samsara*, a Sanskrit word referring to the experience of wandering, trapped through endless cycles of suffering.

The diagram below is a map of the turning wheel of racial karma. The Sanskrit word *karma* and Pali term *kamma*, which gave rise to our modern-day word *karma*, literally mean "action" or "doing." Any kind of intentional action, whether mental, verbal, or physical, is regarded as karma. Karma covers all that is included in the phrase "thought, word, and deed."

This diagram of karma shows how intention affects phenomena in an interconnected cycle of manifestation, transmission, retribution, and continuation. If you are an imaginative learner, you can visualize how it relates to your lived experience.

Karma here means the living power of these three actions of thought, word, and deed to shape the quality of our individual and collective experience. In the Buddhist understanding, karma is not at all a fatalistic doctrine; the Buddha transformed it from the older meaning of cause and effect into a practical understanding of what it means to be conscious of your own intention.

THE WHEEL OF AMERICA'S RACIAL KARMA

The wheel of karma is set in motion by **intention**. This circle starts with what we intend and then manifests in our thinking, our speech, and our behavior. While practicing being more conscious of setting my own intentions in life, I learned a scary thing: our brain is designed to use the least amount of energy necessary to get things done. I'm not just talking about brushing our teeth or driving a car or exercising. I'm talking about deeper things. Unless we make a conscious choice *not* to live on automatic pilot, most of us go through our days without thinking too deeply about the motivations that drive our actions.

Most of us know that changing habits is challenging. How much of what we do is habitual? Studies by neurobiologists and psychologists researching habit formation indicate that 40 to 95 percent of human behavior—how we think, how we respond with emotions, what we say, and how we act—falls into the habit category. So when it comes to deeply rooted thoughts and behaviors, however good we think our intentions may be, without insight about the need to change, the strong resolve to make it happen, and the corresponding action, a good 50 percent of the time we will default to habit.

The second station on this circle is **manifestation**. Whatever we intend gets manifested whether we intend it consciously or unconsciously. Studies show that most of our behavior is unconscious. That's scary to contemplate, but we must. When it comes to our habits around race, we must acknowledge and make what is unconscious conscious, so that we can set wise new intentions as individuals and as a collective. We must wake up.

The third station is **transmission**. The manifestation of our unconscious intention gets transmitted outward into the world through our actions and words as well as inward through our thoughts and emotions. What we manifest, we transmit. We communicate what's on our minds whether we want to or not. We communicate consciously and unconsciously, verbally and nonverbally. Also, very importantly, we communicate through vibration. How did human beings communicate before language? We felt it. Have you ever walked into a room, and when you opened the door you knew, *Boy, somebody was in here a minute ago, and they weren't very happy*? We have this sensitivity, if we haven't let it be educated out of us, this sense of feeling what it is like to be in one another's company. Our mirror neurons fire, building empathy and understanding. Neurologically and evolutionarily, we know we are capable of being together because we are designed to be social creatures.

The next station in this circle is **retribution**. Retribution doesn't mean final judgment. Retribution means the here-and-now consequences of a previous action, because *karma* means "action." Today's adjective for someone who is aware of injustice is "woke"; the quality of being awake to suffering is what defines the Buddha, whose very name means "awakened." If we aren't awake, our retribution won't come in the form of enlightenment.

The last stage after retribution is **continuation**. It's a natural process. If you don't intervene and don't shift the wheel onto new pathways, the wheel of karma simply rolls on. This is true of the modern evolution of racialized consciousness. We see the same heartbreaking patterns repeating again and again: lynching in the deaths of Black people at the hands of the state or slavery in the funneling of Black and Brown people into indentured labor in the prison industrial complex. Karma reveals how our consciousness continues to turn—creating, propagating, cultivating, and systemizing racism worldwide. But every wheel has an axis that sustains its momentum, its movement forward, and its accumulated power. Like the characters in *The Wizard of Oz*, we are journeying with courage, clarity, and heart into the center of the axis, the secret space from which we can heal and transform the suffering of racialized consciousness.

To look deeply into the roots of the social psychology of racism, its colonial aspirations, and the armies that support it, we need to travel back in time to Europe in the 1400s. In the not-too-distant past, intentions of fear and greed were set in motion, unleashing the forces of colonialization and subjugation on the world's peoples and the earth upon which we live. On June 5, 1449, the town of Toledo, Spain, enacted perhaps the first set of racial exclusion laws in modern history against people of Jewish origin, forbidding them from holding office or receiving land from the church unless they could prove four generations of Christian affiliation. Historians like David Brion Davis have described the Spanish categorization and treatment of Jews during the Inquisition as providing "the final seedbed for Christian Negrophobia racism" that "gave rise to a more general concern over 'purity of blood'—*limpieza de sangre* in Spanish—and thus to an early conception of biological race."[1] The concept of blood purity extended from Jews to black Africans, whom Spain and Portugal trafficked in large numbers to the Americas. By the time Colonial-era Virginians and the British entered the Atlantic slave trade in the 1600s, the use of race as a social construct to justify the dehumanization of non–Europeans had been under way for more than a century.

This pattern of political exclusion and suppression of the other-than-white, other-than-pure blood, and other-than-Christian has striking echoes in America today as we imprison families and build a wall at our southern border with Mexico. Our continuous campaigns to obstruct the immigration of Black and Brown peoples clearly reveals the desire to make America as white as possible, in almost complete amnesia of the colonial genocide, kidnapping, robbery, and enslavement of the indigenous peoples of this land we call America.

---

1   Quoted in Jeffrey Gorsky, *Exiles in Sepharad: The Jewish Millennium in Spain* (Philadelphia, PA: The Jewish Publication Society, 2015), 332.

The justification of the European invasion of the Americas and almost all subsequent colonial enterprises can be found in numerous historical documents. Pope Nicholas V first articulated the Doctrine of Discovery in the document fittingly called the papal bull *Dum Diversas* in 1452:

> *We grant you [Kings of Spain and Portugal]*
> *by these present documents, with our Apostolic*
> *Authority, full and free permission to invade,*
> *search out, capture, and subjugate the Saracens*
> *and pagans and any other unbelievers and*
> *enemies of Christ wherever they may be, as*
> *well as their kingdoms, duchies, counties,*
> *principalities, and other property [...] and to*
> *reduce their persons into perpetual slavery.*[2]

Forty-one years later in 1493, Pope Alexander VI issued the papal bull *Inter Caetera* on "the division of the undiscovered world between Spain and

---

2   Alexander Gillespie, *A History of the Laws of War: Volume 1: The Customs and Laws of War with Regards to Combatants and Captives* (Oxford: Hart Publishing / Bloomsbury, 2011).

Portugal,"[3] which played a central role in the Spanish conquest of the New World and supported Spain's strategy to ensure its exclusive right to the lands Columbus had "discovered" the previous year. This fulfilled the spiritual and legal basis for the Doctrine of Discovery, the grand justification for colonization. Once the Catholic Pope in the Vatican did it, then, later on, the Anglicans had to do it in the Americas. They produced their own equivalent of the Doctrine of Discovery.

The shameless certainty of colonial thinking brings to mind the words of author Toni Morrison, who reminds us that we must understand "the very serious function of racism, which is distraction"—a great lie that justifies stealing. That's about the shortest way to say it. The great lie justified building wealth at the expense of someone else's suffering.

Creating wealth. Creating power. Grabbing land. Race was a great smokescreen while all this happened. There have been hundreds of analyses of the subject of race and American history, but for me, this

---

3   This and all other papal and official Catholic church decrees can now be found online on the website papalencyclicals.net.

is a religious scandal. We need to talk as a nation about what's underneath the history and the politics, because until we deal with what's at the root of suffering on a spiritual, psychic, and emotional level, it will continue.

I want you to understand I'm talking about a natural, organic process. The Doctrine of Discovery established a spiritual, political, and legal justification for the colonialization and seizure of land not inhabited by Christians. That definition released soldiers, ministers, missionaries, and merchants across the world to colonize others, imagining this as the fulfillment of their life's glory. What makes this a religious scandal is that it's a lie about the sacred nature of a human being. It denies the reverence for life at the heart of all religions—that the divine is embodied in all humans, including those who don't look like me. That's a lie about the cosmos.

Let's take a longer look at the psychological intent carried many, many years ago by the authors of the racial constructs. For 246 years, from 1619 to 1865, slavery was legal in America. Then, as we all know, it took another hundred years to end legal segregation. You have to understand this was all about the money—and the fear of losing money and privilege—for white American people to stand by and witness this drama for hundreds of years.

Responding to online criticism of the looting that ensued after the police murder of George Floyd in Minneapolis in May 2020, journalist Jenée Osterheld put it like this: "I hate that the livelihood of business owners is burning. But so are Black lives. And we know America's love language is money."

Have you realized that you have been designed as an economic piece of the puzzle? When did our value as human beings become equated with how much we produce and consume? I don't like to think of myself as a consumer. Who decided that's what I was? How did we become not only a market economy but a market culture, in which everything and everyone is monetized? If economics becomes the primacy of your life, what follows is insatiable greed. I once watched a panel with Harry Belafonte, Chris Hedges, and Noam Chomsky on progressive thinking in the United States. One of the questions was, "It seemed like we were making progress. Then we started to go sideways. What happened?" Harry Belafonte said, "We underestimated greed."

In Buddhism, greed or craving is one of the three poisons. The three poisons of ignorance, greed, and aversion are the primary causes that keep sentient beings trapped in repeated cycles of suffering. It's this addiction to pleasure or the illusion of pleasure, this craving for material signs of the worth of my humanity. As Francis Weller says, "The idea that you have to earn a living is a tragic way to think about being a human being." Especially if that's your only way of thinking about your one precious life. This is why the current state is a scandal. It's not just because of what happened in the past. It's because what happened is still happening. Karma is living energy that gets manifested in economics, politics, and the justice system.

We see white people losing it whenever they're faced with the fragility of whiteness because the shadow of privilege is this: You don't learn to take care of yourself inside. You don't learn to value your internal life. You get so fixated on your external life that you forget your internal life is much, much bigger, much deeper, and much more rewarding.

In *How to Hide an Empire*, historian Daniel Immerwahr notes how after World War II, the United States moved away from colonialism toward devising a new sort of influence via innovations in technology and culture, which did not require the control of colonies. The overarching intention to dominate and control was and is still present. The USA was a business that tried to become a country, and in the process, human beings had to become economic units.

You don't understand this country if you don't understand how we have collectively hidden our shame about our greed in our culture. Otherwise, you're living in a commercial. A commercial for the American Dream, the dystopian flipside of which is a nightmare. We think our crisis is the loss of happiness, but it's the destruction of meaning. The crisis is one of people losing their sense of meaning in life and not being able to recognize their own belonging. Part of what you see going on with neo-Nazis, the alt-right, and all these other white nationalist groups rising around the globe has to do with not knowing how to belong.

When our house in Idaho was bombed by members of a white supremacist movement, there was no investigation by local law enforcement and no resolution. It wasn't even reported in the local newspaper.

Nothing happened. It was an encounter with the deep silence of shame and denial surrounding race. I decided to look into that group, which turned out to be a faction of the Aryan Nation. I found myself coming to understand the perspectives of those individuals who were young, brainwashed, confused, and sent out to do harm. This was not long ago, by the way. When we tell this story, people ask, "Well, was that in the 1960s?" No, it wasn't. It was in 1996.

In July 2019, a photo circulated of three young white men with automatic rifles standing around the memorial sign marking the site of Emmett Till's death. The memorial had been shot at continuously and was riddled with bullet holes; in fact, it had been vandalized so often that it had to be replaced within a few weeks of it being installed. Once you start something, it takes on a life of its own. Collective karma means they can't let it go—they cannot or will not let it go.

In October of the same year, a ceremony was held to install a new bulletproof sign. "Okay, you want to shoot it down? We're going to put it right back up," said Airickca Gordon-Taylor, Emmett's cousin. "You're never going to forget about Emmett Till and that he was here. Our family has never received judicial justice from the state of Mississippi for Emmett's murder, so, in some form, this is us saying, 'Until you do right by us, basically, you're never going to forget.'"

We are going through the circle of karma, carried by the momentum of actions in the past that create the present. America's racial karma is a living reality, not a concept. If we don't face ourselves and learn how to practice looking at our actions, we'll never heal.

One of the things I want to say to people of European ancestry is this: I spent three years studying spirituality with a Celtic shaman, and I highly recommend you also explore your native traditions. If you don't know anything about your own roots or don't have access to a body of knowledge and lineage that is nature-centered, powerful, and reverent of life, you may be prone to going the wrong way. Why did that indigenous European wisdom, that tradition with all its beauty and mystery, get cut off? You can go and look at the church. I know everywhere I've been in Mexico and Guatemala, all through Central America and other parts of the world, the cross came, followed right behind by the sword. Chris Hedges calls it "a trail of blood and gold."

As "a nation of immigrants," the United States is home to many who are cut off from their ancestral roots and traumatized by the past. People had permission to kill and to steal, to go against the foundational commandments of their religion. The word used politely was "conquest." That means to kill whoever you need to kill with impunity, whoever stands in your way. I had somebody come up to me recently and say, "I can't believe my ancestor did that. I can't find the space in myself to hold the idea of that cruelty being perpetrated by my ancestors." But we must remember we are dealing with human nature.

This is what we must understand, or we're not going to ever get out of this mess. We have to read the great book called Human Nature. Or rather, The Laws of Human Ethics, which you can find in all the major religions and secular humanism too. Your spiritual practice is to understand why you're doing what you're doing. What's driving you to do that? And to have the courage to ask yourself, "Is that wise? Is that healthy? Will that create suffering?"

The shortest simple example of how we respond to atrocities is our response to genocide and slavery.

There are three stages of avoiding the heartbreak of recognizing the way we perpetrate wrongs. We do something, we deny we did it, and then we forget we denied it, and so it never happened. Or, we say, "Well, I wasn't alive back then." Yet, we have the seeds of our ancestors within us.

Where do you think you came from? Their genes run through your genes. Their blood is in your veins, and our healing has to get that deep, or we will keep passing on our shadow intention to the next generation. One of the insights of Carl Jung is: when our shadows are repressed for a long time, when they get pricked and they emerge from the dark, they come out primitive, as nonlogical entities.

There's no conversation to be had with them. Thich Nhat Hahn liked to say, "Most of the things we *think* will not help us face the beast in humanity." What I know is, I can face the beast in humanity if I have faced the beast in myself, and that brings me profound stillness. So, I am safe to be with myself in the midst of my sorrow, pain, glory, genius, and talent. I can be with myself, and because I can be with myself, I can be with you. Even if my heart is breaking every day.

I'll share a phrase from Martin Luther King Jr. here in conclusion: "Beloved community is our only salvation." For me, beloved community includes the whole planet of beings. To learn how to be together in deep, deep ways. Not in contrived ways around maps and national boundaries but as humans living on this planet as a family with all of nature. When we fly, we look at the surface of the Earth and see that there are no lines. Where are the lines? Only in our collective agreements and intentions, which then become real through our actions.

But these things you already know in your unconscious mind, waiting to manifest like seeds in the dark. I'm just here to encourage you to remember what you know and to put that remembrance into practice. That deep remembrance of who and what you are—beyond borders, beyond categories, in deep belonging in our beloved community—is our salvation.

Part Two

❉

Deeper

I tell you, somebody stole my face.
I can't seem to stop this river of tears.
Black face on the ground, black face in the cages.

I tell you, somebody stole my face.
When I found it, it was dark like the night in its
    elegant beauty.

When I found it, it was in a dreadful theater called
the White Man's Burden. When I found it, it was
already condemned to live in a basket of lies.

But when I found my hidden face, the window of
    eternity swung open.

I tell you, somebody stole my face, my precious face.
I hold it in my hands, catching tears of sorrow and joy.
I hold it with the kind hands of my ancestors.
I hold it turning into many faces,
    appearing across time and space.
I hold it dancing with the cosmos itself.

I tell you, somebody stole my face.
But I have a secret for you, my friend.

Somebody stole your face, too.

I know you've been searching for it.

Find your face.

Find the ground of no coming and no going.

Embrace yourself.

Love yourself.

Lift yourself up so you can lift all the rest of us to
higher ground.

And remember,

when you touch your face,

George Floyd can no longer have that joy.

2
Manifestation: The Making of a Racialized Consciousness

Mind is a field
in which every kind of seed is sown.
This mind-field can also be called
"all the seeds."

THICH NHAT HANH

❧

As the wheel turns, intention, now planted in our minds like a seed in the ground, begins to grow. The Buddha was a practical man who used everyday language to convey his knowledge of the mind to his students. Karma is a wheel, and all thoughts, perceptions, and phenomena are seeds of potential, manifesting in the consciousness. He often spoke of the mind having a fundamental subconscious level, what he termed *alayavijnana*, a storehouse of seeds. This consciousness stores the sense impressions of previous experiences, which form the seeds of future karmas. By paying attention to certain elements of latent potential and not to others, we alter the course of our lives as individuals and as a collective. As Thich Nhat Hanh puts it, "There are both wholesome and unwholesome seeds in our mind-field, sown by ourselves and our parents, schooling, ancestors, and society."[4]

When we fail to recognize and forget to cultivate the seed of our shared humanity, we are in danger. Here, we touch the next spoke of the wheel, the phase of manifestation, in the making of a racialized and divisive consciousness. In nourishing the self-esteem of the intender, the thinking, speech, and behaviors of racialized consciousness became animated in the hearts and minds of many. With careful tending, the seed of racialized intention began to take root as the mind of white superiority.

---

4   Thich Nhat Hanh, *Understanding Our Mind: 50 Verses on Buddhist Psychology* (Berkeley, CA: Parallax Pres, 2002), 25.

"There are three kinds of conceit," the Buddha says. When we think ourselves to be better, equal, or less than someone else, we are trapped in conceits that separate us from each other and cause suffering. The classifying, comparing mind builds and preserves entire superiority, inferiority, and equality complexes. We may believe that there can be conceit only when we think ourselves to be better than someone else, but there can be a kind of pride in self-denigration, or a habit of needing others to be no more than equal. When we uphold ourselves, and make ourselves important, while we compare ourselves, this is conceit.

None of those conceits can in any way describe the mystery, depth, and greatness of my life or yours. We must live as whole people. Deep people. Not simply defined by political conceits.

When Robin DiAngelo's book *White Fragility* came out, the term "white fragility" really caught me by surprise. I was like, *How could you be fragile? You're supposed to be in charge. What the hell?* I mean, if you want to know fragility, grow up with me in Cleveland, Ohio, where I learned how to deal with my fragility as an introverted young person of color; or drive through

Alabama and Mississippi in the 1960s being chased; or find nooses outside my window.

But white fragility and white tears are in fact displays of invulnerability. With the white fragility some of you may be experiencing, you need to understand it's not personal. There is a nonpersonal dimension to your experience of discomfort. As DiAngelo points out, it is unlikely that anyone can be magically exempt from a lifetime of racist conditioning in this system. Fragility and discomfort are not empty, separate cells. They are full of hope, fear, sadness, and desire. Discomfort is not even possible unless we have some notion of what it means to be comfortable in our skins.

The manifestation of racialized consciousness as white supremacy weaves a deadly pattern through human history over the course of five hundred years of social psychology. One of the ways of weaving such a fabric is the presentation and manipulation of powerful images. Images seed the mind, stir emotions, and influence behavior. Years ago, I encountered a small red book by the British-American economist Kenneth E. Boulding, *The Image,* and was inspired by his insight into images and human behavior: "The image lies behind the action of every individual. It accounts for the growth of every cause."[5]

It's important to remember that the images underlying our reality today are hundreds of years old. One of the pioneers of scientific racism was Carl Linnaeus (1707–1778), the Swedish physician, botanist, and zoologist. He is celebrated for his work on the taxonomic bases of binomial nomenclature for fauna and flora. It was he who biologically defined the *human race* and named us as *Homo sapiens* in 1758. His classifications of humanity still imprint our imagination, illustrating the power of images and implied story.

Nine years before the founding of the United States in 1776, Linnaeus's 1767 book *Systema Naturae* labeled several varieties of human species. In *Homo sapiens,* he proposed four taxa or categories: *Africanus, Americanus, Asiaticus,* and *Europeanus,* based on place of origin at first and later skin color: black Africans, red Americans, yellow Asians, and white Europeans. Below are a few of these descriptions, illuminating the power of image craft.

---

5   Kenneth E. Boulding, *The Image: Knowledge in Life and Society* (Ann Arbor, MI: University of Michigan Press, 1956), 28.

- *Homo sapiens africanus.* Black, phlegmatic, relaxed; black, frizzled hair; silky skin, flat nose, tumid lips; females without shame; mammary glands give milk abundantly; crafty, sly, lazy, cunning, lustful, careless; anoints himself with grease; and governed by caprice.

- *Homo sapiens americanus.* Red, ill-tempered, subjugated. Hair black, straight, thick; nostrils wide; face harsh, beard scanty. Obstinate, contented, free. Paints himself with red lines. Ruled by custom.

- *Homo sapiens asiaticus.* Yellow, melancholic, stiff; black hair, dark eyes; severe, haughty, greedy; covered with loose clothing; and ruled by opinions.

- *Homo sapiens europeanus.* White, sanguine, browny; with abundant, long hair; blue eyes; gentle, acute, inventive; covered with close vestments; and governed by laws.[6]

It isn't much of a stretch to see how this pseudoscientific cacophony of beliefs without empirical evidence continues to impregnate our minds and

---

6   From Dorothy E. Roberts, *Fatal Invention: How Science, Politics, and Big Business Re-create Race in the Twenty-First Century* (New York: The New Press, 2011).

contribute to the fabrication of white racial superiority and its privileges. Even though this is a list of several racial groupings, we can see the binary thinking of superior–inferior humans revealed in these descriptions. There's one good group, and the others are all, well, "other." Jonathan Marks, professor of anthropology at the University of North Carolina at Charlotte says, "race science emerged in the context of colonial political ideologies, of oppression and exploitation. It was a need to classify people, make them as homogeneous as possible."[7] Grouping people made it easier to control them, dehumanize them, and ultimately justify the entire colonial mind.

The economic, political, and cultural impacts of colonial thinking went hand-in-hand with peculiar notions such as, nonwhites don't feel pain like white people do, which fed the historic American disregard of black people as fully human. Founding Father Thomas Jefferson famously mused, "Their griefs are transient. Those numberless afflictions, which render it doubtful whether heaven has given life to us in

---

mercy or in wrath, are less felt, and sooner forgotten with them."[8]

The manifestation of racialized scientific race-craft can be found throughout Eurocentric education and literature. Entire books and dissertations have been written on the topic, but let's take a look at one prime example, a hundred years after Linnaeus. In the first stanza of the 1899 poem "White Man's Burden" by Rudyard Kipling, to many the epitome of colonial writing and thinking, we find at first glance that this poem appears to be a response to the Philippine–American War, which encouraged the United States to assume colonial control of the Filipino people and their country. However, within the poem are images describing the nonwhites as if they were a unique species "half-devil and half-child" to be held captive and saved by the nobility of the white race.

> Take up the White Man's burden—
> Send forth the best ye breed—
> Go bind your sons to exile
> To serve your captives' need;

---

8   Thomas Jefferson, *Notes on the State of Virginia* (London: Penguin, 1998), 146.

To wait in heavy harness,
On fluttered folk and wild—
Your new-caught, sullen peoples, ·
Half-devil and half-child.

In a cartoon drawn to match the poem, the United States, depicted as the figure of an exhausted Uncle Sam, can be seen trudging after Britain's John Bull, his Anglo-Saxon partner, carrying nonwhite nations—all depicted in grotesque racist caricatures—uphill from the depths of barbarism and over the rocks of brutality, vice, superstition, ignorance, and oppression to the heights of civilization.

The cartoon captures the arrogance of the white superiority myth as it obscures the devious intent of the colonial paradigm, instead highlighting the white man's burden to civilize all the uncivilized.

When we consider how we now say the United States was built on the backs of enslaved people, the thinking behind such carefully crafted caricatures seems delusional at best. It is time to lay such fantasies to rest, yet they persist in more subtle forms. What lies behind the attachment to fixed beliefs of racial type and supremacy?

Cartoon by Victor Gilliam, *The White Man's Burden (Apologies to Rudyard Kipling)*,
April 1, 1899

Any visit to the social media conversations of young
people growing up in the United States today reveals
that the reduction of human beings to physical types
via racial classifications is very much alive, animating
not only discussions around beauty, intelligence, and
self-worth but basic guarantees to shelter, safety, and
life itself. The race-crafters, who are as industrious as
ever in the twenty-first century, continue to raise the
question: Are all of us human or not?

3
Transmission: The Race Wave

Elite white bodies invented and institutionalized
the myth that the white body is the supreme
standard by which all other bodies' humanity
are measured. Then they blew much of their
trauma through the bodies of Africans and
their descendants—and made lynching into an
American spectator sport. This served to embed
trauma in Black bodies, but it did nothing to
mend the trauma in white ones.

RESMAA MENAKEM

❧

A few hundred years ago, presentations of race
emphasizing white superiority became their
own European cottage industry, much like some parts

of today's media, with its scholars, pundits, and inter-lopers confirming the superiority of white-skinned humanity. The racialized intent of this karmic wheel reached a new stage of momentum of transmission or communication.

The karmic stage of transmission is "the rise of race" as it's referred to in *The Lies That Bind* by Kwame Anthony Appiah. By the nineteenth cen-tury, in the world of the North Atlantic, the "racial fixation" was everywhere. But this consciousness did not occur by accident, nor is it the outcome of divine intention; it is the direct result of the intent to permit greed for domination, backed up by militarism. White supremacy became the defining criteria for self-worth, accumulating wealth and power through subjugating others and the natural world.

Images and beliefs around race have permeated the academy and the institutions of Western educa-tion. The sciences and humanities of the eighteenth century were rife with the racialization of conscious-ness given legitimacy by religious leaders, academics, and anyone who wanted to assert their right to power. This racial fixation insinuated itself within the psychological and social fabric of the world.

This wave produced clever, diabolical ways of institutionalizing common derogatory images and code words for nonwhite non–Christian otherness, which continues to this day. While it is not unnatural for us to fear what we do not know, this is different because it is the intentional nurturing of fear-based stories in the minds of individuals and the policies of society.

America's racial karma is transmitted in the intellectual creation of a hierarchy of racialized consciousness, passionate orations of white superiority, anti-otherness publications, and movements supporting white racial superiority. Successfully transmitted anti-otherness was now popularized and fueled by kitchen table discussions and backroom treachery. These behaviors have been embodied in customs, laws, and communities throughout the United States, on the one hand claiming equality and on the other, denying nonwhites a sense of belonging in this country.

Redlining in the United States and other discriminatory practices specifically deprived nonwhite Americans of homes. When Peggy and I went to close on our first house together twenty-five years ago in Idaho, in reviewing the documents I was stunned by the Covenant, Conditions, and Restrictions section of the contract, commonly known as CC&Rs, which restrict what homeowners can and can't do with their property. Property was supposed to be passed between white men only. I, of course, questioned this and would not proceed without a change in the language of the contract. The second stunning thing was when the paperwork was complete and ready for my signature, I noticed there was no place for Peggy to sign. Women were also not worthy of homes either, apparently. Again I stopped the process until this was also corrected. This felt like a personal wake-up call, showing me how white superiority started in the Eurocentric patriarchal mind.

Lest you think this is some anecdote from the distant past, in 2019, Zoe Ann Olson, executive director of the Intermountain Fair Housing Council, Inc., described this insidious pattern of racialized consciousness in American real estate:

> *About a year ago, a homebuyer came into my office and showed me the CC&Rs for a home that he wished to purchase that was part of a homeowner's association. He was shocked to see that one provision said, "No persons other*

*than persons of the White race may reside on
the property except domestic servants of the
owner or tenant."*[9]

The momentum of the superior-inferior race construct found adherents as it reached beyond Europe
and crashed upon shores all over Planet Earth. Stereo-
types of nonwhites were transmitted widely through
the media and imbedded and imprinted on the American soul. In the 1857 Supreme Court case *Dred Scott
v. John F. A. Sanford*, Chief Justice Roger B. Taney
dismissed the humanness of those of African descent
and decreed that the full rights and privileges of the
US Constitution did not belong to Black Americans.
This legal ruling, so recent in our history, was the legal
backdrop to a popular culture that reduced nonwhite
Americans to caricatures, at best ludicrous and at
worst evil, as we saw in the "White Man's Burden"
cartoon. Ghastly images proclaiming, "The Chinese
Must Go!" jostled with cartoons of the Cuban people
needing to be fed American values as medicine to

---

9   Rachel Spacek, "'No Persons Other Than Persons of the White
Race': Racist Language Remains in Older Homes' Documents." Idaho
Press. November 05, 2019. Accessed June 19, 2020.

make them well enough to rise from barbarism (the same rhetoric rolled out again in this century's wars in Iraq). The intent to promote racialized hierarchy was on full display. Anyone shocked by American racism in 2020 needs to spend some time studying history and understand that the imprints of the past are still present in our consciousness, like seeds waiting for just a little watering to grow.

Study racism and don't look away. Understand how it works. We can see here the karmic action from intent to manifestation to transmission implanting the seeds of ideas of racial superiority in our hearts and minds with its mission to subjugate nonwhites. Note your physical and emotional responses and scan your mind to see how these implanted images hide in your consciousness too.

This transmission stage of the wheel, having extended itself to the New World, accelerated the worldwide making of a Eurocentric, Anglocentric identity as the white race. It stirred a fresh sense of pride, privilege, and power to make the world over in its own image. It conveyed the message of the Doctrine of Discovery as it inspired the idea of white nationalism as America's destiny.

The successful transmission of racialized consciousness at the roots of America's foundation affects us all whether we know it or not. There is no hiding from the wheel's tracks visible in the lands stolen, lives lost, and backs sold insuring pride and profit. The truth of the matter is an inversion of the white man's burden of carrying Black and Brown bodies to the salvation of true civilization. We know America was built on the backs of slaves and founded on the bodies of the first peoples of this land, but many still find difficulty in accepting such facts because they go against the American Dream narrative. We have spent the last five hundred years becoming so skillful in denying our atrocities and projecting the shadows of America's racial karma onto the bodies of nonwhites that we are like people suffering from traumatic brain injuries and amnesia.

Ta-Nehisi Coates's book *Between the World and Me,* presented as a letter to his adolescent son, tells the story of violence against Black bodies in the American landscape as an American tradition. The American police officer

carries with him the power of the American

state and the weight of an American legacy
(a legacy which gave them a strange birthright;
the right to beat, rape, rob, and pillage the
black body), and they necessitate that of the
bodies destroyed every year, some wild and
disproportionate number of them will be
Black. In America, it is traditional to destroy
the black body—it is heritage. And, because
it is heritage, the destroyers will rarely be held
accountable.

Trauma lives in the body. How do I know America's racial karma is still alive in me? I know because of my body's experience of living in this racialized society. Hearing the word "race" still sends shivers up my spine and makes my stomach tighten, and my mind's defense mechanisms go on high alert.

How about you? What do you feel when you discuss race? I say this because this book may be activating you or making you more conscious of your physical sensations around race. If discomfort arises, good: it means you are alive. Bring your attention to your breath as it is, let it be as it is. It may help to focus on the rising and falling of your abdomen as the cycle of your breathing moves through your body. Feel your body's weight on the earth; feel the earth's stability as you relax your breathing. It means you are touching the roots of your humanity—your precious body.

4

Retribution: Consequences, Shadows, and Portents

Where there is sorrow,
there is holy ground.

OSCAR WILDE

❧

The word "retribution" has religious overtones, but in our conception of karma and retribution, it's important to first remember that retribution is a natural occurrence in daily life. We may leave something in the oven too long or short a time, and it doesn't come out good. When I worked with flowers, people frequently brought me orchids almost dead from overwatering, and of course, we may underwater a plant and it dies. We live in a world of interactions and effects.

The human crisis at the center of our earth's crisis is a profound example of the fluid, dynamic nature of retribution. Some of the effects of America's racial karma are immediate, and others have festered in the caves of our hearts and lingered in the halls of our institutions, but there is no escape. Even our skillful denials and habitual forgetfulness cannot save us from the effects of this historic transmission's consequences, shadows, and portents.

The socially embodied Eurocentric model of humanness as superior and its resulting display of racialized consciousness is bound to have shocking retributive effects within ourselves and society. Retribution here does not mean vengeance or the final judgment at the end of our lives. It means that the effects of the wheel of racialized consciousness are recognizably present in our lives. It is rather a dynamic interplay between the scars in our bodies and souls of five hundred years of a profound human catastrophe. We live with the economic, political, and cultural patterns imprinted in our psyches and their active residues in our communities and institutions. We are in sociological despair, meaning we are as a nation out of alignment with our depth of humanity.

I walk today with a contorted movement as my body continuously adapts to my old knee trauma. America's racial karma's effects are just like that. As a human family, we have lived a contorted existence since the Europeans landed on these beautiful shores.

But our racial contortion is transformable because race is a human invention—an invention that nevertheless has physical effects. The advances in the last twenty-five years in brain sciences have provided profound insights into how humans are biologically impacted by trauma, and it's now understood there is a wide range of different types of trauma. Humans share brain systems of the fear response with other mammals, birds, and reptiles. Fight, flight, or freeze: we can see all of these in effect in relation to racial trauma. These systems have been evolutionarily preserved because fear helps protect us from danger, injury, and death.

The kind of trauma I am speaking of goes beyond common notions of trauma caused by physical events such as medical emergencies, violent crimes, and the effects of war. Trauma is a biological response to the shock and fear of experiences of unsafety, threat, and harm. I view our patterns of trauma adaptation rather as affirmations of our biological vulnerability and our ability to grow as conscious living systems responding to our experience.

Humans are a remarkably resilient species, but traumatic patterns persist over generations. Dr. Bessel van der Kolk, author of *The Body Keeps the Score*, says, "... whether on a large scale (on our own histories or cultures) or close to home, on our families, with dark secrets being imperceptibly passed down through generations ... they leave traces on our minds and emotions, on our capacity for joy and intimacy and even our biology and immune systems." These traces of trauma are the underlying web of our secret interactions with one another alienating us from our sense of empathy and shared humanity.

We often deny or are numb to these sensations, especially in matters of race. The problem is, when they subside, we think they have gone away, when in fact they have become somaticized and stored in our bodies. Our traumatic memory capsules can be triggered by real or imagined threats and open up highly reactive behaviors that may be obvious or hidden. We have developed elaborate ways to escape feeling our shared racial anguish.

Our bodies hold the retribution energies of America's racial karma. No one escapes this fear and trembling deep in our bones. Whether we were or are victims, perpetrators, or witnesses, we are unavoidably biologically destabilized or dysregulated by our sensory experience or the memories of it. There's a growing body of thought and research on the cross-generational transmission of trauma. We have also learned much in the last twenty years about the powerful effects of the impacts on human development of cross-generational trauma as well as adverse childhood experiences (ACEs).

Researcher Joy DeGruy-Leary offers a powerful illumination of the traumatic effects of America's racial karma in her work on posttraumatic slave syndrome. She says, "While African Americans managed to emerge from chattel slavery and the oppressive decades that followed with great strength and resiliency, they did not emerge unscathed. Slavery produced centuries of physical, psychological and spiritual injury." There has been a movement for some time to have racial trauma included in official clinical diagnosis manuals; we've seen that the psycho-biological impact of crimes on nonwhite persons has been hidden, dismissed, or covered up.

Retribution is the full force of this karmic wheel's revelation. We are living with the reckoning of the racialization of humanity that paved that trail of blood and gold. It not only resides in our bodies as unprocessed biological trauma, it has also permeated our individual and social psychology, rendering the latter completely bankrupt. Americans are in social despair from the absence of genuine connection.

How do I know genuine connection creates safe spaces to heal and be ourselves? To heal ourselves from what? From the grief of experiencing life alone, in this land of shadows we call America. By aloneness, I mean a sense of disconnection and disassociation from the whole of our collective life force—a nagging feeling of fragmentation with one's whole self and the whole of our society.

We become whole again by embracing our grief. Our grief work is probably the most important thing we can do at this time of awakening as a society, to heal the places in us and in our country that have not known love. Every town, every home, every person needs to experience being loved to overcome our deep alienation and despair. Psychotherapist Francis Weller says in his book *The Wild Edge of Sorrow*, "There is some strange intimacy between grief and aliveness, some sacred exchange between what seems unbearable and what is most exquisitely alive."[10] The grief of racial trauma is such an opening, a gateway to healing America's racial karma.

REFLECTION

The Places That Have Not Known Love

Where are the places, people, and potentials in America that have not known love? What comes to your mind as you contemplate this question?

REFLECTION

Ancestral Grief

Weller describes one gate to healing as *ancestral grief*: "This is the grief we carry in our bodies from sorrows experienced by our ancestors. Much of this grief

---

10   Francis Weller, *The Wild Edge of Sorrow* (Berkeley, CA: North Atlantic Books, 2015), 1.

lingers in a layer of silence, unacknowledged." When you contemplate America's racial karma, what ancestors, stories, and silences are you aware of?

※

The silences in ourselves and our families are like scar tissue over our wounds. There is a post–World War II memory from France that my father shared with me. He wanted it kept private because of the tears that would inevitably come. When US soldiers and German prisoners would board a train, he told me, all the white people would share the same seating, and African American soldiers were relegated to the caboose. I can still feel his heartbreak as he realized his denigration, the lack of honor or even regard from those he had fought beside to cast him aside so arrogantly.

We continue to devise ways and means to hide from what has happened to our hearts and minds because of the wheel's success in shaping our consciousness, institutions, communities, and the American way of life. We hide in business, circumspection, and defiance—both passive and aggressive in our attempts to secure the reality of being a participant in, and beneficiary of, America's racial karma. Our legacy is we live in the sea of a tragic story of what it truly means to be human.

It is important to remember that, as described in *The Atlantic* by J.M. Berger in 2016, this shaping of America's racialized consciousness affects our human conditioning, personal and collective, formal and informal.

> *White nationalism was the law of the land in the United States through most of the country's history. In the wake of the Civil War, institutionalized white supremacy began to erode, a process that accelerated into the twentieth century. Against the backdrop of the Civil Rights Movement, white nationalism began to develop complex ideologies, with a number of different strains emerging. Pedestrian racism—simply disliking or discriminating against people based on race—still played a significant role in society, but as mainstream white nationalism became increasingly stigmatized, these ideological variants became subcultures in which violent extremism could fester.*

As I thought about our American racialized conditioning and how to describe its continuing retribution, it occurred to me that Western civilization has known the importance of education in conditioning the mind for a long time, literally millennia. Plato's *Republic* uses the allegory of the cave to illuminate how we create our reality. "Let me show ... how far our nature is enlightened or unenlightened. Behold! Human beings living in an underground den ... here they have been from their childhood, and have their legs and necks chained so they cannot move."[11] The prisoners are in the dark with no means of light or communication, watching shadows projected on the wall before them from a fire behind them, which they take to be their reality. Now, in the United States, we are like these prisoners, subjected to a barrage of images of the world via our education and culture, which are provided by puppeteers we cannot see behind us.

We are imprisoned in fictions, which appear to be our reality. This is the wizardry of America's racial karma passed from generation to generation through

---

11   Plato's *Republic* from *Dialogues of Plato,* translated by Benjamin Jowett, (Cambridge: Cambridge University Press, 2010).

the actions of thinking, speaking, and physical behaviors. Our very constitutional history contrives it, our lived suffering testifies to it, and our cultural indifference gives permission for the retribution to continue.

Our social conditioning and education have been the agent of transmission of racial superiority, and if we are to change America's racial karma, we must dismantle the hierarchy of races with whites at the top. Our education to be human determines how we are human.

5
Continuation

I tell you what freedom is to me: no fear.

NINA SIMONE

❋

Ten years ago, when I started holding the Dharma talks that would eventually turn into this book, the title I had in mind was *America's Karma*. At some point it became *America's Racial Karma*. The more I look, I see there's no separation between the two. There is no America without racial karma.

You cannot understand this place without knowing the history of economic power in the United States and how it was abused. You cannot begin to heal this place if you don't understand that. By this place, I mean this place that is America in you and

America in me because as touched on, we now know through our research in epigenetics that trauma can be cross-generationally transmitted. We know this is true with patterns of incest and other forms of abuse. Our suffering is in our genes! This is not a political topic at that level. This is a human topic and our willingness to go deeply into our own humanity is our only solution.

Now, self-identifying in certain categories is not a problem. I like who I am. I like being Black. I am fine identifying as he/him. I think it's cool, but I'm not confused about the mental construct that gave rise to the language of ranking and classifying. I'm not confused by the choice I've made not to be caught in that construct. The issue isn't that we still describe ourselves by skin color using two-hundred-year-old definitions, the issue is the *intention* behind that description.

Whether we're talking about our skin-tone spectrum, our ethnicity, our class, our age, or our place on the gender spectrum, if we see ourselves as belonging to a family of humanity, without anyone being higher or lower, greater or lesser than, such distinctions only celebrate our diversity. When there is no belonging to each other, the acceptance of our separation from others and nature is our doom. The purpose of being alive is to discover we're not separate. That takes practice. Spiritual practice. That takes friends from different backgrounds who practice with that same quality of aspiration and consciousness, what in Buddhism is called a Sangha, or what Thich Nhat Hanh and Martin Luther King Jr. called the Beloved Community.

The dehumanization inherent in America's racial karma—from the most obvious and brutal forms to the most subtle—need not continue. Whether we are witnesses or victims, or even perpetrators evoking terror, protected by a conspiracy of white silence, we are trapped when we could be free. How do I know we can be free? Because within each of us exist all the seeds of human potential. The idea of white superiority is just one of those potentialities. But once intended, manifested, and transmitted to humanity, it continues, creating untold human damage.

We are at another fork in our long road toward the wholeness of the peoples in this land. The question posed by this moment is: What human potentials will we nurture, cultivate, and reward?

Do we wish to live forever with white supremacy and white fragility and the experience of disgust and fright? The silence of my 1950s childhood around race has given way to shouts of rage, riots, and civil unrest, yet still our societal power structures stand unmoving. Our dreams lie unfinished, our imagination is devoted to hypervigilance, and our energy is consumed by the restlessness in our bodies with what fears may come. Writing these pages, I learned of the murder of Ahmaud Arbery in Georgia, several months after his death, thanks to a video posted on the Internet. I was chilled to the bone, and body memories of my own narrow escapes from death at the hands of white men came to haunt me.

"Ahmaud Arbery is dead because Americans think black men are criminals," say the news headlines.[12] Shot while jogging in a residential neighborhood by a white father and his son, Gregory and Travis McMichael, with the shooting captured on a cellphone camera by a third white man, this local conspiracy of three seemed to live out the mission

---

12   In an article posted in the opinion section of *The Guardian* by Benjamin Dixon, May 8, 2020.

of slave patrols and catchers in the American South, 155 years after the end of slavery. Somehow, they had received America's racial karma's transmission of the depravity of white privilege to incarcerate, harm, or murder nonwhites at will and without consequence. It was only after the video footage was released to the public that charges were brought against the McMichaels. The entrenched pattern of murder and silent complicity was summed up in a Facebook post: "Always remember, they didn't make arrests because they saw the tape. They made arrests because we saw the tape."

When we look at ourselves in the mirror, we must ask ourselves, truly, is this the America we wish to continue? Do we wish to see the ancient ritual of Black and Brown body sacrifice on the altar of white superiority repeated again and again? What do we make of what lies before us racially in America? More tragedy, or the triumph of new ways of being together?

In the words of trauma therapist Resmaa Menakem, author of *My Grandmother's Hands*:

> *One or two things will happen: Ideally, America will grow up and out of white-body*

supremacy; Americans will begin healing their
long-held trauma around race; and whiteness
will begin to evolve from race to culture, and
then to community. The other possibility is
that white-body supremacy will continue to be
reinforced as the dominant structured form of
energy in American culture, in much the same
way Aryan supremacy dominated German
culture in the 1930s and early 1940s. If
Americans choose the latter scenario, the racialized
trauma that wounds so many American bodies
will continue to mutate into insanity and create
even more brutality and genocide.[13]

I agree with these descriptions of the two likely outcomes given our current conditions. However, a third scenario filled me with fear and trembling for us all. What is the human legacy we wish to leave for generations to come? Will it be the pitiful response of indifference?

From the vicious reactivity of those seeking to maintain white dominance, can there be the

---

13   Resmaa Menakem, *My Grandmother's Hands: Racialized Trauma and the Pathway to Mending Our Hearts and Bodies* (Las Vegas: Central Recovery Press, 2017), 1.

daring invention of a new humanness within and beyond race?

Healing and transforming the patterns of continuation in our internalized racialized karma depends on a fresher and deeper understanding of our humanity. To realize this understanding is beyond information gathering. It is a journey of lived experience, and it is a spiritual matter, not to be confused with religious belief. It is a matter of embodiment of the profound. This possibility of healing and transformation depends on body-centered spiritual practices and training that can heal the axis of the wheel itself. How might we begin to heal ourselves at these deeper levels of consciousness that still create and sustain the wheel of America's racial karma? That is the invitation of this moment.

Part Three

＊

Deeper Still

A Meditation on Ancestors

Relax into the working ground of your ancestors.
Look within with a clear mind.
Watch as memories, thoughts, fears, disappointments,
  anger, and wonder flow by.

Breathe …
Receive a spacious heart and let what is most vivid
  melt away into holy emptiness.
Hold onto nothing and yet embrace everything, as
you fall into the river of goodness hidden in your
bones, flowing toward the ocean of strength, forgiveness, and grace.

6
The Axis of the Wheel

Radical simply means
"grasping things at the root."

ANGELA DAVIS

❧

As precious humans, we have within us deep
impulses, instincts, and energies. These potential
seeds of intention may be latent or hidden, and do not
escape our evolutionary wiring and historic conditioning. The wheel of America's racial karma is fueled by
such energies, which must be faced if we are to heal.
Only if we—and here we are looking at our white
friends—are able to do the inner work as well as the
outer work to heal this debilitating legacy of racialized
suffering will we emerge from the current period.

Of course, it is urgent, necessary, and a worthy task to transform our social practices, policies, and systems of institutionalized race consciousness. But it is more than evident to me that oftentimes such aspirations are frozen, paralyzed, and sabotaged by a spiritual crisis, a crisis of a poverty of inner work blocking our deep insight, resilience, and potential for deep systemic change.

In Buddhist psychology, our natural impulses and instincts coexist within the individual and collective conditioning of our bodies, hearts, and minds in a flow of processes of consciousness. As we touched on earlier in our discussion of manifestation in chapter two, these metaphorical seeds exist as energies in what we term our store consciousness, that is, all of the information from the past, from our ancestors, and all of the information received from the others. This means they are primary sources for our thinking, speaking, and physical behaviors. If we are to heal our racialized bodies, hearts, and minds, and the systems of this land, first we must learn to understand the power of our minds. After all, the political and judicial systems we live in were created by us; they mirror our minds in every way and act as networks in our collective body politic much like the physiological systems in an individual human body.

We must learn how to manage our deep mind of the racialized seeds within, through active recognition, vulnerable acceptance, fierce naming, and the selective cultivation of the energies to which we give our life force.

It is very important to remember that when I speak of "mind" in this book, I really mean body-mind, for our lived experience is nondual. Body and mind are two sides of the same coin, and what happens to one happens to the other; what manifests in the body also manifests in the mind, and vice versa. In Thich Nhat Hanh's book *Understanding Our Mind*, which explores the Buddha's teachings on psychology, he describes the qualities of seeds of the mind. We are to envision the mind as a great field in which every kind of seed is sown. I like to imagine a field of wildflowers. This image of the mind as a field or garden speaks to me of beauty, generativity, and change. The neurosciences have coined the term *neuroplasticity* for this quality of flexibility and dynamic growth at the neurological level.

Within us are an infinite variety of seeds: seeds of suffering, happiness, hatred, delusion, jealousy, joy, kindness, justice, greed, forgetfulness, and enlightenment. The seeds of racialized consciousness are also present in our internalized trauma, racial perceptions and names, and our social habits. The seed of racialized consciousness and its karmic effects are part of the very fabric of American life, so much so that many don't know how to breathe outside the climate of white supremacy. How sad a retribution that is.

These seeds or potentials manifest themselves as a living presence in the individual and collective thinking, speech, and behaviors fueling the turning of America's karmic wheel. These seeds are all stored in our deepest consciousness. Some seeds are innate; others are handed down by our evolutionary and immediate biological ancestors. Some were sown while we were still in the womb, others were sown when we were children. Very importantly, whether transmitted by family, friends, society, or education, all our seeds are, by nature, both individual and collective. These seeds or possibilities are in what is called "store consciousness," the reservoir, the warehouse, or museum of our individual and collective consciousness. The quality of our lives individually and collectively depends on the quality of the seeds that lie deep in our consciousness.

We are blessed with a brain and nervous system that possess qualities of neuroplasticity: the ability for the brain's neurons to learn, adapt, and change, and we thus always have an opportunity to nourish the aspects of our consciousness that are joyful, wise, and free. Thich Nhat Hanh calls the process selective watering. We water the seeds we wish to grow—the seeds we need for a future worth living—and we don't water the toxic seeds. So, when we resolve to heal, we can and must rewire our racialized consciousness and rearticulate an embodied depth understanding of our shared humanity.

The healing of America's racial karma at its deepest levels will require deeper education, skillful introspection, and wise cultivating of the seeds of compassion for self and all relations. It will require identifying the seeds of prejudice, bigotry, and indifference to racial suffering and removing the nutriments that cause them to grow. We can begin with enhancing our emotional intelligence and stability through processing internalized trauma and deepening spiritual practices of resilience. It will also require a new commitment to our wholeness. It is bold and enlivening work to untie the racial knots of suffering within our bodies and minds.

This means developing the skills to tend to our hearts' gardens by identifying, recognizing, calling all seeds by their true names, and facilitating the acceptance that begins the healing process. We accept the truth that we live a life in which we can water, cultivate, and grow nonracialized seeds in our mind. As I go about my daily life, I continually ask myself: If I give this seed more energy where will it take me? Will it lead to wholeness in self and society? Will it lead to a safe and just society? Will it lead to meaningful, sustainable lives for all of us? This is step one in recognizing the wizard of race inside ourselves and not contributing to its continuation.

The second step is learning the art of healing *mana*, a Buddhist Sanskrit term that may be translated as "arrogance" or "conceit." Linked to the discriminating faculty of the mind, it sorts incoming sensory impressions and presents them to our consciousness. Mana grabs stimuli as evidence that we are separate selves, and when it is afflicted with unwholesome, poisonous seeds of ignorance, greed, and hatred, it is a reactive, swollen mind that makes whatever it can grasp be the foundation of its pride and nourish its imagined value.

Deeply seated in the depths of our store consciousness is this idea that there is a self that is separate from others, a self somehow independent from all else, what we may call "non-self elements." The function of mana is to cling to store consciousness as a separate self. For mana, any foundation will do; we can find its footprints in positions of power, in the bravado of wealth and status as well as the subtle myth identifying a special class of superior belonging. This wizardry is like a virus always seeking a host to embrace it while it constructs the basis for discriminating against others.

It is not difficult to see the embodied characteristics of mana in the tracks left by the wheel of America's racial karma. We read descriptions in Buddhist texts that illuminate mana as the wizard force behind white supremacy. The Dhammasangani (1116) says:

> *What is the fetter of conceit? Conceit at the thought "I am the better man"; conceit at the thought "I am as good (as they)"; conceit at the thought "I am lowly"—all such sort of*

*conceit, overweening conceitedness, loftiness,
haughtiness, flaunting a flag, assumption,
desire of the heart for self-advertisement—this
is called conceit.*

The mana of racism is characterized by haughtiness, self-praise, greed dissociated from needs, being driven by self-promoting opinions, and exhibiting the constant need for self-referencing to validate its being. It is a form of lunacy caught in racial reification of that which only exists in the realm of mythology. At a simple social-psychological level we can witness this fancying of whiteness in the global market for skin-lightening products that is valued in billions of dollars annually.

Our work is to heal our store consciousness of tendencies to diminish ourselves and others and to plant and mindfully cultivate our most positive human seeds. Mana obscures our attention to the seeds of goodness and enlightenment within us. It puts our empathy and generosity to sleep. Mana is not the enemy, but if it is not tamed it can become monstrous. When our natural sense of self-cherishing becomes afflicted with the three poisons of greed, hatred, and delusion, we can become monsters.

However, when mana is healed and transformed, it nourishes our wisdom, helping us see all things as ultimately connected in the nature of what my teacher Thich Nhat Hanh calls *interbeing*. As a species, we are in desperate need to learn to recognize when our natural tendencies for self-cherishing are hijacked by the three poisons of greed, hate, and delusion. If we don't, we will continue to sow seeds of racialized consciousness in the world.

American culture is not generally recognized as reflective but rather adolescently powerfully reactive, holding onto the belief that America's inherent goodness will prevail, even when faced with live footage of state brutality. The conceit of American virtue survives the shooting of schoolchildren, the killing of millions of civilians from Vietnam and Iraq, and the installation of a president armed with scripts of slogans to keep the shadows of greed, hate, and delusion alive. This habitual reactivity and denial have until now prevented collective deep reflection on the depths of our racialized consciousness. Many of us are caught in cognitive dissonance—emotionally and spiritually bypassing the profound existential implications of our racialized consciousness and its continuing trance permeating our social lives. We have continued to give psychic energy to white supremacy and its horrors, while we have not as a nation chosen to cultivate our deep shared humanity.

I shudder when I contemplate what has been lost. May we recover our humanity and create a future yet imagined. Let us grow up into our full human wholeness. As we act to make changes to our institutions at the deepest levels and broadest scale, in our conversations and meditations, it is my hope that we can transform our consciousness and take steps on the healing journey that I call crossing mercy's bridge.

7

Crossing Mercy's Bridge:
Healing the Wounds of Time

We are here to awaken
from the illusion of our separateness.

THICH NHAT HANH

❧

The bridge of mercy lies deep within us and among us, however well it is hidden by clouds of conflict, cruelty, and hatred. I know this to be true when I bear witness to my own life experience. I come from mercy; I exist because of it. I was adopted at the age of eight months by a Christian couple, Roy and Viola Ward. Circumstances could have made this young family homeless, but we took refuge in the attic of Marion and Ollie Tindal, who offered my parents shelter in their home and extended the grace of their mercy to us. I went on to become their grandson, and my parents would go on to adopt three more children, who would become my siblings.

Mercy's bridge rests on the solid foundations of human evolutionary resilience, brain neuroplasticity, and spiritual awakening. Our species' wiring for compassion and the desire to eliminate our racialized suffering provide the real potential for our social imagination to grow.

I was overjoyed when I first came across the figure of the goddess of mercy in Buddhist traditions, because I had already experienced her presence as this living energy fully embodied in my life. My mother, Viola Paris, was an embodiment of the energy of mercy in everything she did.

Mercy is, first, offering a safe space for those who appear to be other. How do I recognize when I am in such a space? Well, my body relaxes, I feel at ease, and my nervous system is no longer in a state of hypervigilance. In a safe space, I am nourished by the taste of being welcomed just as I am, with my skin just as it is, and all my gifts and talents can reveal themselves with joy, encouraged and supported enough to learn and grow. We feel beloved. While I can share many stories of gratitude toward mercy's bridge in my personal life, the invitation of this book is to invite us all to cross mercy's bridge.

This land we call America has been anything but a safe space. Healing ourselves is difficult because the racialized wounds of time in this society are, in fact, unforgivable. It seems that as a culture we take great pride in our capacity to be unmerciful.

You may say upon hearing this, "I am not like that!" This is a response conditioned by individualism, with its consequential dissociation from being together in the stitches of our social fabric. Look at the prison system in America if you want an example of our collective fragmentation: the United States has the highest rate of incarceration in the world, with 2.3 million people in prison, and of those people, one-third are people of color.[14] This could not happen in a society of merciful people guided by justice and integrity. Like it or not, we as individuals acquiesce to America's racial karma daily. Our rampant devotion to

---

14   See Michelle Alexander's *The New Jim Crow: Mass Incarceration in the Age of Colorblindness* (New York: The New Press, 2010).

individualism has allowed us to hide from acknowledging our historically ever-present tragedy.

We need the experience of what I call deep mercy. Mercy lies in our mindful actions of thinking, speech, and behaviors toward ourselves and one another. We may not seem as if we are capable of collective deep mercy, as expressed in acts that restore a sense of shared humanity with one another. Yet these acts of mercy are not absent; in fact, they are the invisible web that sustains living connection and progress in human history. We have survived as a species by crossing its bridge again and again.

And now we must make another historic crossing to consciously journey from the quicksand of afflicted self-cherishing, the grasping, clinging, and attachment of mana that is the axis of the wheel of America's racial karma. The racialized bodily habit energies living in our hearts and minds are not indestructible objects; they are the results of intentions embodied individually, collectively, and systemically. The spiritual and social work of healing America's racial karma requires a new conscious intent of living together in individual and collective safety, wellness, justice, and profound meaning. Who wouldn't want that?

I still remember attending my first seminar on Black Heritage and White Racism in 1970s Chicago. It was a mix of Black and white adults learning together over several days of discussing race in America. It was unsettling to be with strangers energized by the barely contained emotional charge of fear, anger, and grief combined with the discomfort of our social conditioning. It was a very good experience that led to more programs like it, which have evolved into today's diversity and inclusion trainings. However, looking back now, I realize this is where I witnessed the power of unprocessed trauma and its paralyzing effect on any significant change in our relationships with one another. Today's White Awareness and People of Color affinity groups have a better chance of moving through the frozenness of the past with the tools of trauma resiliency to help them.

Mercy's bridge is kept alive by the energies of deep justice flowing back and forth, the truth of suffering beyond the constrictions of the law. It is the justice of our precious bodies being respected and loved concretely as divinely human. However many rituals of forgiveness we may perform, if they do not touch the storehouse of racial afflictions in our consciousness, they offer little to me because even forgiveness is not forgetfulness. Mercy means to surrender cloaking ourselves from ourselves and experiencing a shared vulnerability that we've likely never felt before. It invites surrendering the fateful silence of centuries robbing us of our own humanity.

It is an invitation to cross thresholds of healing so our racialized consciousness may become profoundly humanized, to care for ourselves and our planet. We are each connected to one another in ways that support the growth of our healing capacities. We have forgotten so much of what can heal us, right here, right now. Our collective heritages are filled with remedies beyond the veil of the colonial heart and mind. These healing thresholds are already with us inside our body-mind and all around us, above and below.

REFLECTION

Self-Compassion and Posttraumatic Growth

On the bridge of mercy, the first threshold to cross is compassion. Among emotion researchers, compassion is defined as the feeling that arises when you are confronted with another's suffering and feel motivated to relieve that suffering. In taking a deeper look at the etymology of the word "compassion," we find *com* (with) and *passion* (feeling)—*compassion* means to suffer together. Compassion is more than a natural impulse or a seeded potential of caring within us; it can be cultivated. In the context of America's racial karma, compassion begins with a skillful practice of self-care. Compassion is openness to our lived human experience down to our toes. It is learning to live beyond pretense and returning to the bodily experience of being human in America.

This is the openness to deep change. It is an invitation to recover our right to empathy. It is creating enough space within to hold the light and shadow of America's racial karma without being destroyed by it, because you are healing and releasing the traumatic memories in your body of ages of your ancestors' innocent suffering as well as your own.

Indicators exist of wholesome growth as internalized racialized traumas are released. Those previous energies of suffering now become the fresh, flowing energies of resilience. A powerful shift in perception and perspective emerges as our deep human consciousness gains strength and neurological patterning occurs. This means the capacity to consciously withdraw both psychic energy and systemic support from continuing America's racial karma has taken root.

As shared in religious and philosophical teachings for thousands of years, it is evident that trauma can lead to positive change. No mud, no lotus. But it wasn't until the mid-1990s that the term posttraumatic growth was coined by psychologists Richard Tedeschi and Lawrence Calhoun. Their studies show healing tends to occur in five general areas:

1. Sometimes people who must face major life crises develop a sense that new opportunities have emerged from the struggle, opening up possibilities that were not present before.

2. A second area is a change in relationships with others. Some people experience closer relationships with some specific people, and they can also experience an increased sense of connection to others who suffer.

3. A third area of possible change is an increased sense of one's own strength—*If I lived through that, I can face anything.*

4. A fourth aspect of posttraumatic growth experienced by some people is a greater appreciation for life in general.

5. The fifth area involves the spiritual or religious domain. Some individuals experience a deepening of their spiritual lives; *however*, this deepening can also involve a significant change in one's belief system.

Map these aspects of posttraumatic growth to your own lived experience and see if any are true for you. I can offer the following examples from my life:

1. Appreciation of life. For me this has led to a deepening gratitude for my life; greater mental stability; enjoying less reactivity to unpleasant triggers of anxiety and fear; and, most precious of all, dwelling in a peace and joy unshakable.

2. Relationship with others. I consider myself blessed to have lived, worked, served, and met so many wonderful people the world over. I have been touched again and again by beauty, intelligence, creativity, sincerity, and kindness. This has been challenging as my introverted tendencies are strong, but I have been healed in so many ways by these precious encounters. I am learning to embody the mind of love, for it is where equanimity is born, and to extend loving kindness and creativity outward and to look at all beings with the eyes of compassion.

3. Discovering new possibilities. In Carl Jung's book *The Undiscovered Self,* he was asked after World War II

what the future would bring. "Only by understanding our unconscious inner nature—'the undiscovered self'—can we gain the self-knowledge that is antithetical to ideological fanaticism," he writes. But this requires facing the duality of the human psyche—the existence of good and evil in us all, or in Buddhist terms, our wholesome and unwholesome seeds. In my meditations and reflections I realized that in the undiscovered self is the undiscovered society; this means that our external life is intractably bound to our inner life. This is the underlying insight of this book. It means it is possible for us to come home to our whole being, to heal ourselves and engage in life-affirming social imagination and inspiration.

4. Greater experience of life in general. Through this long journey, my personal strengths have continued to grow as well as my love of learning and my capacity to inspire and be inspired by others. I have learned how to hold my suffering with grace and embody the self-affirmation of noble qualities within me.

5. Consciousness shifts happen. I find myself now with deeper awareness of life's meaning. I have realized that I am the Earth; she is not separate from me or any of us. Thanks to my beloved teacher Thich Nhat Hanh, I understand that the peace and happiness of the entire world, even the peace and happiness of my

ancestors in the world of the dead, depends on my own peace and happiness.

Without the conscious cultivation of resilience and neurological change, we will continue to fail at being a whole people. How can we have justice if there is not justice within ourselves? Our American collective consciousness lives in fragmentation. If enough of us heal our sense of fragmentation and dissociation from one another, we have a real chance of a different future. We can create and energize new ways of being together filled with vitality, imagination, and joy.

We can see that many Americans hold and express disdain toward the idea of healing our racialized consciousness. In fact, both our history and the daily news indicate even at this present moment that there are those among us who will disrupt, destroy, and kill based on difference alone. When the energies of our natural and precious self-cherishing become addicted to greed, hate, and delusion, a racialized political view of the world is born.

I cannot tell you how to heal, but I can share with you how I have healed my racialized consciousness and continue to do so through meditations, exercises, and learnings even while being immersed in environments of hatred. There is power in practicing applied mindfulness with a focused attention on healing our racialized consciousness.

Healing takes time. When you cut off a fan, it keeps running for a while before it stops because of its previous momentum. In the same way, the turning of the racial karma wheel may keep going, but when we cut off the fuel to it—when we stop feeding it with hatred and instead, by nourishing our self-love, our self-compassion, and our joy, this karma will end and our society will change. Some of you may be familiar with mindfulness practice, which is a path to living a non-superficial life, a life of giving wise attention to our human experience so we may heal and transform the suffering within ourselves, between ourselves, and among ourselves. And as we take steps on that path, our capacity for deep compassion and clear wisdom becomes fully embodied in us.

Get Help Now

As you cross the bridge of mercy and begin to do the work of healing, you may discover moments of emotional difficulty and physical unease. Do not worry—the healing capacities are already within us. They have just been hidden by our social patterns of denial and busyness, masking the fear of not knowing the skills to heal the inner life, which unintentionally perpetuates America's racial karma. Accustomed to living in a place where there is no mercy, we may dread falling short and failing, not realizing that falling into our inner space of healing is what we need to do.

To move through our fear, first let us bring our nervous system into balance. The risk incurred when leading ourselves out of the prison of racialized consciousness feels frustrating and exhausting. The following are "Help Now!" strategies from the Trauma Resource Institute, where I trained, which can help us stay within our zones of emotional resiliency.[15]

Help Now! strategies are ten quick, simple, practical, and easy-to-remember activities to engage the senses (designed to build your resiliency when you're either too amped up or too checked out to be available for yourself due to stress). At times when meditation practice in daily life might feel overwhelming, try these tips to get back into your body.

Help Now! activities can be helpful as you go through your days. They are not for de-escalating high-stress situations when you may have a legitimate reason to feel unsafe. Rather, they are for when you are in a low or high point in your feelings and want to help regulate your nervous system into a more balanced state by getting in touch with your body and your mind.

When we're feeling anxious, we need to dial down our stress response, so we don't get freaked out. This is not a sequential list but a menu of choices—read

---

15   Visit the website of the Trauma Resource Institute (traumaresourceinstitute.com) for supportive materials and information on Help Now! strategies.

through them and pick one at a time and pra
the strategy.

1. Drink a glass of water, juice, or a cup of tea.
2. Look around the room or space wherever you are, paying attention to what you notice.
3. Name six colors you see around you, indoors or outdoors.
4. Now close your eyes slowly; then open them slowly after a few seconds; now look around the space again.
5. However you are able, move around the room counting backward from 10, 9, 8, 7, 6, etc.
6. If you are inside, examine the furniture and touch the surface, noticing if it is hard, soft, smooth, or rough, etc. If you are outside, focus on the sense of gravity beneath your feet; find a tree to lean against, or hug; if near water, stick your hands in, noticing your physical sensations.
7. Notice how your skin senses the temperature wherever you may be.
8. Turn attention to noticing the sounds around you.
9. If you're inside or outside, walk and pay attention to the movement of your arms and legs and how your feet are contacting the earth.
10. Push your hands against a nearby wall, door, or tree, noticing your muscles acting. Or, stand and reach your hands and body toward the wall or tree.

Check in and sense how you feel afterward. Each small action is a small reset of the nervous system toward balance.

Coming Home to the Body Each Morning

I have trained myself to wake up slowly each morning, enjoying the stillness, letting myself awaken and sense my embodiment. I pay attention to the sensations of my breathing and slowly scan my body and mind part by part, noticing where there may be tensions or tightness in the body or emotions from dreams hanging in the air. Try it! Instead of jumping and rushing into the day, practice slowing down and relaxing any hypervigilant habits you may have accumulated.

After this, I focus on the Five Remembrances meditation from the Buddhist tradition. These remembrances can be easily misunderstood as a statement of fatalism, but they are simple everyday experiences. The Five Remembrances are a statement of my freedom to respond to life's experiences with humility, respect, and compassion.

The Five Remembrances

The act of remembering clears our negative karmas and compels us to act with integrity in the present. I practice this version of the Buddha's Five Remembrances offered by Thich Nhat Hanh in the Plum Village chanting book,[16] but you may find affirmations from other traditions resonate with you. I breathe and contemplate these verses, giving five or seven breath cycles to each verse.

Say these verses slowly, sensing the words resonating in your body, letting whatever thoughts, images, or stories float by like clouds in a blue sky, without analyzing or interpreting them. Let them rest until they shift and pass away. Stay with your breath and observe the body's sensations under all your thinking.

❁ I am of the nature to grow old. There is no way to escape growing old.

❁ I am of the nature to have ill health. There is no way to escape ill health.

---

16   Thich Nhat Hanh, *Chanting from the Heart: Buddhist Ceremonies and Daily Practices* (Berkeley, CA: Parallax Press, 2007).

- I am of the nature to die. There is no way to escape death.

- All that is dear to me and everyone I love are of the nature to change. There is no way to escape being separated from them.

- My actions are my only true belongings. I cannot escape the consequences of my actions. My actions are the ground upon which I stand.

This practice grounds me in my human experience beyond racialized labels. Here, I touch and am touched by the fragility of human life as well as its preciousness. Through this daily practice, I find freedom from racial reactivity. I have been able to see myself as an Earthling on a planet with other Earth beings. I continue to experience deep relief from the clinging to racialized images of myself and others. I now experience myself as nature-defined, an inseparable part of the Earth itself, not simply defined by human mental constructs. I see and sense the energy I have spent denying and hiding from the basic reality of earthly existence. A new and deeper vitality is now available to me to create myself and the world anew.

Greeting the Day

Once I am up and ready, I greet the day outside of my four walls whenever I can. I walk slowly to a chosen spot where I feel safe and grounded. I can feel my connection to the earth beneath my feet. I again check in with my breath, noticing its qualities without judgment. Is my breathing easy, or is it labored? Fast cycle or slow? Whatever the breathing pattern, I receive and give thanks for the miracle of the breath. Then, I do a gradual 360-degree turn, facing the sun and feeling its warmth penetrating all sides of my body. I also notice the other sensations on my skin. I listen quietly to the sounds of the world. I am especially fond of being with birds, trees, mountains, rivers, and other earth creatures.

How does this heal racialized karma? When I am in the natural world outside, I am moved by the experience of being nonjudged and unharmed by the politics of my skin. I told a friend recently that I have never been disrespected or intentionally caused to suffer by a tree or a rock. I touch the wonders of life daily, and in doing so, I nourish my heart and mind with the flow of beauty, vastness, and gratitude as they rebalance wellness in my nervous system.

Cultivating Resources of Resilience

These practices have been key for me in continually healing myself from racialized trauma. At the Trauma Resource Institute where I trained, I learned a practice called *resourcing*. The practice of resourcing is a skill of resilience. It is a capacity intuitively present already within us. A resource is a person, place, activity, or memory that empowers you with a sense of safety, stability, strength, inspiration, creativity, and support. A resource may be a concrete present moment, one from your personal history, or real or fictional characters from books and films, etc. A resource can be anything that helps you feel better. It can be something the person likes about him/herself, a positive memory, a person, place, animal, spiritual guide, or anything that provides comfort. Through continuous practice, you can establish, embody, and return to a space of wellness within. Skillful resourcing can shift our nervous system from distress, discomfort, and overwhelm to a greater sense of balance and well-being.

To practice conscious resourcing is simply to make a short list based on the above. Make a list of resources. You can ask:

- What gives you strength and/or joy in your life?

- What uplifts you or makes you feel calm or peaceful?

- What or who inspires you to heal America's racialized karma?

Choose one resource to practice with. Activate your sensory awareness and positive experiences with this resource and give mindful attention to sensations that are pleasant or neutral inside the body. Then come to a rest, noticing anything that may have or have not shifted. You may want to make some journal notes.

REFLECTION

Opening the Working Ground of Race

This is a reflective exercise to understand how the energies of America's racial karma are alive in your life story. Find a place where you may stop to reflect mindfully. You may speak, write, think, and meditate on these questions. If you write, keep your thoughts in a journal so you may read them again. What insights do you gain from going deeply into your storehouse of thoughts, feelings, and memories about race?

* What is the story of how your name came to be?

* When did you first notice differences in people's looks?

* What stories about race and skin color did you hear growing up?

* What phrases do you use to describe racial differences?

* How is your body responding to this exercise?

* How is your body responding to these memories?

* What race seeds were planted as you look back over your life? Seeds meaning thoughts, words, actions, and events that remain with you, consciously and unconsciously.

* Which of these seeds were wholesome (leading away from racialized hate, greed, and delusion)?

* Which of these seeds were unwholesome (leading toward racialized hate, greed, and delusion)?

* Which seeds are most impactful in your life now?

* What is your priority in healing the racialized consciousness in yourself?

Mindfulness and Recognizing the Seeds Within

The practice of present-moment wise attention is critical for tracking our racialized seed energies. I have found that seeds of fear, disappointment, and fury exist alongside non-racialized seeds of kindness, community, and joy in the storehouse of my mind. This mindfulness practice helps me stay current with my total wellness. These seeds may be stimulated to arise at any time from the storehouse it seems, due to conditions and events individual or collective. What is important to remember is what arises is not your enemy, because it is you. The practice is to create space within ourselves so that our seeds can present themselves for de-nourishment or increased nourishment.

1. When racialized consciousness is present, the practitioner knows it is present.

2. When racialized consciousness is not present, the practitioner knows it is not present.

3. The practitioner investigates and knows the causes of this racialized seed arising.

4. The practitioner knows how to hold this presence of suffering.

5. The practitioner knows how to expand their attention to their whole body-mind by mindful breathing, creating a safe space within so that suffering is not pushed away nor does one drown in it.

PRACTICE

Holding Suffering with Clarity and Grace

When the gates of grief open in my heart, and I am overwhelmed by the continuousness of blood on the ground, there are a few things I can do. Many years ago in Plum Village I heard a poem by Thich Nhat Hanh that he wrote after a bombing that happened in Vietnam during the war. A bombing by Americans. He wrote:

For Warmth[17]

I hold my face in my two hands.
No, I am not crying.
I hold my face in my two hands
to keep the loneliness warm—
two hands protecting,
two hands nourishing,
two hands preventing
my soul from leaving me
in anger.

It is very important here to understand the point of anger in Buddhism. Anger is a normal, perfectly human experience that you and I may be having in daily life, but especially at this moment in relation to race. The point of anger is not to lose ourselves—not to lose our sense of integrity; not to lose our sense of loving; and not to lose ourselves in fragmentation.

The strong emotion could be anger; it could be fear; it could be numbness; but the point of practice

---

17   From Thich Nhat Hanh, *Call Me by My True Names: The Collected Poems of Thich Nhat Hanh* (Berkeley, CA: Parallax Press, 2001).

is not to lose ourselves. We don't push away suffering. We feel every ounce of suffering through our whole body, but we don't drown in it either. And that's the great practice of my life.

Strong emotions lay things bare for anybody who was unclear. For anybody who is addicted to disassociating from other people's suffering and pain, it is surely time to grieve their losses.

Recently I heard the poem sung as a song by my friend Betsy Rose, and I was so moved by its simple grace that I began a practice of holding the heartbreak of grief in my two hands.

You can play a song or any music that is meaningful to you. I find a quiet spot—even the car will do. I get as comfortable as possible and put on the song while holding my precious face in my two hands, and I make time to cry. Grief moves through me and at the end I take some time to relax.

To overcome injustice, we must not lose our centeredness, our spiritual resilience, and most importantly not our capacity to respond with wisdom, compassion, and action in creating a new world.

8
The Call to Ancestorship

❦

My prayer for us is the tears flowing down the bottom of my heart, watering the ground, broken by shock and grief and remembrance of the fallen and of those yet to fall in the sea of suffering.

My prayer is to stand upright in the house of great belonging, this miraculous pearl, this true land of my birth. My prayer is to speak the sound of the great drum of the open heart and follow the thunder that is the truth.

It is time to unbind ourselves from these shadows. It is time to go deep as we face the mirror of ourselves. It is time to go to the river and be washed and cleansed in the holy flows of the energies of love and kindness, compassion, joy, equanimity, and imagination, trusting that the great river will carry us home.

We must understand our sorrow at this time as divine energy and not simply as the result of political error. The gate of ancestral grief is being flooded in all of us. Only by practicing and acting well now can we heal our ancestral trauma and become ancestors worthy of being descended from in the future.

We recognize our interconnectedness with our collective body as Americans. I am a drop in the ocean, but I'm also the ocean. I'm a drop in America, but I'm also America. Every pain, every confusion, every good, every bad, and every ugly of America is in me. As I transform myself and heal and take care of myself, I'm very conscious that I'm healing and transforming and taking care of America.

So, my spiritual practice is to help me deal with the disappointment, the frustration, the fatigue, the anxiety, the overwhelm, the panic, and the hypervigilance that come with living in the United States and being part of its collective insanity. My experience has been that every time I leave the country for more than a week and come back, I'm retraumatized. I wish I wasn't, but I am, and so, I'm happier to be in the cradle of the mountains who don't know my name or care, who don't know my race or care; or the magpies that I can talk to or the birds that I sing with in the morning or the wind that blows through without any name, any classification, any category; and I'm held up like you are by the natural world.

Notice in yourself how the racial hierarchy has affected you and your nervous system. Observe not only your thoughts, but also, how your body has been responding. Have you noticed your own hypervigilance? Have you noticed your own fatigue? Have you noticed your own sense of overwhelm, or panic, or even hopelessness? All these issues, feelings, and sensations rise in us, but shame also rises in us. It's the shame of not being valued as a human being. It's the shame of the experience of not being worthy of love. This is our work, this is my work as an elder in my community, to witness and transform our collective experience of the pain of the last five hundred years, so that it will no longer continue to be transmitted.

I spent a day in silence for George Floyd. I found it healing. One of the ways I practice with my own trauma is to let it be, not try to fix it. Trauma must be respected, because it is part of our precious humanness. We can experience wanting to fight or flee or just numbness. We may experience the paralysis of not knowing what to do. This is our biological system in action. It is normal, and there is nothing wrong. In fact, you might say something is right if we are experiencing this fear, this anger, this numbness, this heartbreak.

I use poetry to practice resourcing myself. I dabble in writing poetry, and I also enjoy the poetry of others.

I spend as much time as I can outside of the four walls of my house. I spend time with the birds, chatting with them every morning and every evening. At sunrise I'm outside feeling the warmth of the sun, and at sunset I'm outside with the moonlight. It is very important not to undersell ourselves simply as human defined. We must understand ourselves as nature defined. When we understand ourselves that way, we can touch our generativity, and we can touch our resilience that is beyond time and space.

Singing, music, dance, movement—all of these are ancient practices from our ancestors that many of us have forgotten. The birds remind me of that. And when we think of ancestors, please remember our greatest ancestor Mother Earth. She is filled with energies that can help us heal. She is filled with equanimity that holds us together on this planet.

We have to create communities of resilience. What I mean by that is no one in this country from the very beginning believed we could live together. That's our legacy. And when we truly see and feel what we experience, how could our inheritance be otherwise? We started that way. This is karma. And karma can be healed, and karma can be transformed, but only if we choose to turn the wheel to another track.

This community of resilience is one of kindness, openness, generosity, sanity, and love. There are so many people in this land who do not believe this is possible. So, we are figuring it out. It won't be neat. It will be messy. I know it has to be concrete; it has to be embodied so that when people encounter it, they feel it, and they can speak about it.

I am practicing right now with some mantras. The first one is, "Stand up in the house of belonging." Don't act like this is not your land. Don't act like you can't take charge because it's obvious to me that the principalities and powers who are supposed to be in charge of this land at this moment are absolutely incapable. So stand up! Act like you are a real human being. Don't let the messengers of systemic racism define your life for you. Don't let them define your power for you.

The second is, "Take your seat at the table of healing and transformation." I'm thinking of the words of my grandma, Marion Tindall. She said, "Don't let some fool take your seat." Take your seat. Be present and care for yourself; love yourself. As you love yourself and care for yourself that love will move outward. It will spill out all around you with a fragrance of holiness.

The third mantra is, "Ride the winds of change, unafraid." Act like the mighty ones of old, who knew no fear. Embrace their wild resilience and their vision of what is really possible for us together in America's racial karma.

Selected Readings

Alexander, Michelle. *The New Jim Crow: Mass Incarceration in the Age of Colorblindness.* New York: The New Press, 2010.

Appiah, Kwame Anthony. *The Lies That Bind: Rethinking Identity.* New York: W. W. Norton, 2018.

Boulding, Kenneth E. *The Image: Knowledge in Life and Society.* Ann Arbor, MI: University of Michigan Press, 1956.

Coates, Ta-Nehisi. *Between the World and Me.* New York: One World, 2015.

We Were Eight Years in Power: An American Tragedy. New York: One World, 2017.

DeGruy-Leary, Joy. *Post Traumatic Slave Syndrome: America's Legacy of Enduring Injury and Healing.* Milwaukie, OR: Uptone Press, 2005.

DiAngelo, Robin. *White Fragility: Why It's So Hard for White People to Talk About Racism.* Boston, MA: Beacon Press, 2018.

Fields, Karen E. and Barbara J. Fields. *Racecraft: The Soul of Inequality in American Life.* New York: Verso, 2012.

Immerwahr, Daniel. *How to Hide an Empire: A History of the Greater United States.* New York: Farrar, Straus, and Giroux, 2019.

Menakem, Resmaa. *My Grandmother's Hands: Racialized Trauma and the Pathway to Mending Our Hearts and Bodies.* Las Vegas: Central Recovery Press, 2017.

Nhat Hanh, Thich. *Chanting from the Heart: Buddhist Ceremonies and Daily Practices.* Berkeley, CA: Parallax Press, 2007.

Reconciliation: Healing the Inner Child. Berkeley, CA: Parallax Press, 2006.

Understanding Our Mind: 50 Verses on Buddhist Psychology. Berkeley, CA: Parallax Press, 2002.

O'Brien, Gail Williams. *The Color of the Law: Race, Violence, and Justice in the Post-World War II South.* Chapel Hill, NC: University of North Carolina Press, 1999.

Roberts, Dorothy E. *Fatal Invention: How Science, Politics, and Big Business Re-create Race in the Twenty-First Century.* New York: New Press, 2011.

Weller, Francis. *The Wild Edge of Sorrow: Rituals of Renewal and the Sacred Work of Grief.* Berkeley, CA: North Atlantic Books, 2015.

Work, Robertson. *A Compassionate Civilization: The Urgency of Sustainable Development and Mindful Activism—Reflections and Recommendations.* North Charleston, SC: CreateSpace, 2017.

Young, Damon. *What Doesn't Kill You Makes You Blacker.* New York: HarperCollins, 2019.

Acknowledgments

I offer sincere gratitude to my teacher Zen Master Thich Nhat Hanh and the Plum Village community; to Hisae Matsuda, Earlita Chenault, Ebonie Ledbetter, and the staff of Parallax Press for their support of my voice. To the many friends, Lotus Institute board members, students, colleagues, and supporters who have encouraged this publication through offering venues for talks at Many Faces Sangha, Philadelphia; Shree Yoga, Taos; the Mindfulness Community of Puget Sound; the Minneapolis Zen Center; East Bay Meditation Center, Oakland; the Blue Heron Sangha in Columbus, Ohio; the Insight Meditation Center in Seattle; the Asheville Zen Center; the Unitarian Universalist Fellowship in Vista, California; and the Vista Buddhist Temple. I know these were labors of love.

I offer unspeakable thanks to my parents, Roy and Viola Ward, who adopted me at eight months and my grandparents Marion and Ollie Tindal, who adopted all of us into their life. They taught me that it's possible to love a stranger. Thank you for teaching me compassion and joy, for honoring my uniqueness, and introducing me to a spiritual life.

And none of this would have been possible without my beloved wife, Peggy Rowe, and her love, bravery, and unwavering support for my life's creativity.